When All God's Children Get Together

MERCER
UNIVERSITY PRESS

Endowed by

TOM WATSON BROWN

and

THE WATSON-BROWN FOUNDATION, INC.

When All God's Children Get Together

A Memoir of Baptists and Race

Emmanuel L. McCall

Mercer University Press
Macon, Georgia

MUP/P365

978-0-88146-065-0

First Edition.

Books published by Mercer University Press are printed on acid
free paper that meets the requirements of American National
Standard for Information Sciences—Permanence of Paper for
Printed Library Materials.

Library of Congress Cataloging-in-Publication Data

McCall, Emmanuel L.
When all God's children get together : a memoir of Baptists
and race /
Emmanuel L. McCall. -- 1st ed.
p. cm.
Includes bibliographical references and index.
ISBN-13: 978-0-88146-065-0 (pbk. : alk. paper)
1. Baptists—United States—History—20th century.
2. Race relations—Religious aspects—Christianity.
3. Reconciliation—Religious aspects—Christianity. I. Title.
BX6237.M33 2007
286'.1750904--dc22
2007016934

Contents

vi

Prologue

"When All God's Children Get Together"

When all God's children get together,
What a time! What a time! What a time!
We're going to sit down at the Welcome Table,
What a time! What a time! What a time!

When preachers and deacons get together,
What a time! What a time! What a time!
We're going to sit down at the Welcome Table,
What a time! What a time! What a time!

When Black folks and White folks get together,
What a time! What a time! What a time!
We're going to sit down at the Welcome Table,
What a time! What a time! What a time!

When all God's children get together,
What a time! What a time! What a time!
We're going to sit down at the Welcome Table,
What a time! What a time! What a time!

Acknowledgments

This book is affectionately dedicated to the many men and women, both black and white, who dreamed of making Baptists in the South better through racial reconciliation.

There is a special place for the memories of Dr. Victor T. Glass, who directed the racial emphases from 1965–1975 at the Home Mission Board. I succeeded him in directing the department to Dr. Hugo Culpepper, who was my missions professor at The Southern Baptist Theological Seminary, and who later directed the division under which I worked; to Dr. Arthur Rutledge, the president of the Home Mission Board, who initiated the staff position to which I came and gave me freedom and responsibility in fulfilling the job assignment; to my neighbors and colleagues, Drs. W. R. Grigg and Wendell Belew, who both encouraged me and stood with me in difficult times; to Drs. Carlisle Driggers and Edward Wheeler, staff associates whose camaraderie will always be cherished.

I express special appreciation to my wife, Emma Marie, whose love and support has comforted me through the years. She also read, proofed, and typed this manuscript.

My life has been richly blessed because of these and many more.

Preface

For a long time I have been encouraged by Southern Baptists with whom I worked in various arenas of denominational life to write a book about my experiences in racial reconciliation. I had wanted to do so, but from a neutral point of view. I developed a manuscript that simply told the story of how racial reconciliation progressed among Baptists in the South, focusing unknown persons whom I felt made significant contributions. I also focused on events that God used to help reconciliation happen.

The publishers felt that the manuscript would be strengthened if I did an interpretive memoir. I value their opinion. Thus, the story is told from my point of view.

I have attempted to tell a positive story of the progress that has been made between 1957 and 1995. Much is written about the negatives of Baptist race relations in the South. Not much is said about those who effected change. I attempt to tell their stories.

The readers will also know of many persons who are unknown to the writer. I hope you will also find a way to pay tribute to their efforts. We are now in the generation for whom this kind of information is ancient history. Let's help them know about our collective past. Hopefully, they will not duplicate it.

Foreword

In 1976 Dr. R. Pierce Beaver, a University of Chicago missiologist, wrote *American Missions in Bicentennial Perspectives*.[1] In this book, which celebrated our nation's 200th birthday, Beaver called the Southern Baptist Convention (SBC) the most racially and ethnically inclusive denomination in the United States, an observation affirmed by Dr. C. Peter Wagner in *Your Spiritual Gifts Can Help Your Church Grow*.[2] The United Methodist Church's research and survey department also affirmed Pierce's observation in 1986.[3]

In 1990, the Sunday School Board and the Home Mission Board noted that more than 1,500 African Americans were under appointment in the mission agencies. In 1989 African-American churches were among the top ten leaders of baptisms in seven states.[4] Drawing on the information provided by the Annual Church Profiles, Amy Green says there were more than 2,700 African American churches in 2000.[5]

African Americans have been curriculum writers for SBC resources since 1968. They have served as moderators of associations, presidents of state conventions, and staff members of associations and state conventions. Dr. Charles King of

---

[1] R. Pierce Beaver, *American Missions in Bicentennial Perspective* (Pasadena CA: William Carey Library, 1977).

[2] C. Peter Wagner, *Your Spiritual Gifts Can Help Your Church Grow* (Glendale CA: G/L Publications, 1970) 202.

[3] Roy Howard Beck, *The United Methodist Reporter* (Nashville TN) 21 February 1986.

[4] Home Mission Board staff survey, Atlanta GA, 1990.

[5] "Southern Baptist Surprise," *Christianity Today* (September 2004).

Frankfort, Kentucky, was elected vice president of the SBC in 1976. Reverend Gary Frost, Dr. Elijah W. McCall, and Rev. Fred Luter have also been elected vice presidents of the SBC.

How did the above happen in view of the historic Southern Baptist positions regarding race? This book suggests that between 1957 and 1995, God did miraculous things through events, persons, and organizations to change the SBC. Many of those persons have been and will remain unknown to us. Some of them we know. Some events and movements should be celebrated for the changes they effected. I will give exploration and affirmation to them.

Since this is something of a memoir, the reader will hear the story from my point of view. Fortunately, I kept news clips, magazines, books, and other resources from as far back as 1956. As a college student I became aware of the changes that were in progress. I now have two locker trunks of materials from the years 1956–1995.

And, now, my story.

Receiving bachelor's degree from president Duke K. McCall,
Southern Baptist Theological Seminary, 1962

Doing a "tossed salad" for a AJC feature story in the Food section

With State Directors of Racial Reconciliation: Corbin Cooper (NC),
Bob Lovejoy (OK), and Earl Stirewalt (GA); 1976

First Southwide Conference of Baptists for Racial Reconciliation
at Southern Baptist Theological Seminary, 1954

Presiding at the inauguration of Dr. Robert Franklin,
president of the Interdenominational Theological Center, 1996

Welcomed by the mayor of Accra, Ghana, West Africa, 1976

Southern Baptist Theological Seminary commencement with
Dr. Roy Honnycutt as National Alumni President inducting new graduates, 1992

Team partner Dr. Gardner C. Taylor at the Taylor Golf Classic, May 13, 2002

Cynthia Ray (president of Woman's Convention, National Baptist Convention, Coretta Scott King, and Emmanuel McCall at the BWA International Summit of Baptists against Racism and Ethnic Cleansing, Atlanta GA, January 8–11, 1999

(L-R) Roy Medley (executive director American Baptist Churches),
Vincent Wood (president Caribbean Baptist Fellowship), Emmanuel McCall,
David Coffey (president BWA), Denton Lotz (general secretary BWA),
at the 2006 Executive Committee Meeting

Victor T. Glass, Roland T. Smith, and Emmanuel McCall, 1976
(Smith served as special assistant to Dr. J. B. Lawrence, HMB, from 1942–1949;
Glass directed the Department of Work with National Baptists, 1965–1975)

McCall with President and Mrs. Carter at Maranatha Baptist Church, Plains GA, April 2005

McCall with Dellana (executive director of WMU) and Bill O'Brien,
Berlin, Germany, July 29, 1985

Billy Graham, Fred Moseley, Wendell Belew, Emmanuel McCall,
Clarice Whitner (secretary), Ruth McKinney (secretary),
Russell Dilday (pastor of Second Ponce de Leon Baptist), June 1969

Home church, Valley Baptist Church, Wheatland PA

McCall with Dr. Thomas Gilles, leader of Virgin Island Baptists, USVA

Preaching with interpreter Rev. Samuel Akuamobe, "New Life Crusade,"
Accra, Ghana, West Africa, 1976

McCall with Dr. Jimmy Allen, president of SBC Radio & T.V. Commission and the ACTS Advisory Board, programming directed to the Black community

Emmanuel, Sr., Emma Marie, Emmanuel, Jr., son,
and Evalya (Evie) Morris, daughter

In Retrospect

With the advantage of reviewing the flow of my life, I now see the connecting links that appear to be God's preparation for a ministry of racial reconciliation.

I was born in Sharon, Pennsylvania, February 4, 1936, to very godly parents. I actually resided in the borough of Wheatland, an area of steel mills and the attending support businesses.

Many of the African Americans living in a continuing complex of boroughs, villages, and cities had moved to the area from southern cities. Those in Wheatland came from Mississippi, while those in Farrell came from Cheraw, South Carolina. Others had come from Virginia. The Anglos were mostly first- and second-generation immigrants from a number of European countries. Germans and Italians were the dominant group, but there were Czechs, Yugoslavs, Polish, Russians, Greeks, Ukrainians, some Swedes and Norwegians. Many lived on farms. Those who lived in the cities and villages usually lived in community enclaves. Interspersed between those enclaves were often Jews and African Americans. The conflicts that went on were between ethnic groups, not races. African Americans and Jews were sometimes the buffers between ethnic groups. I did not know racial prejudice until I left Wheatland at age seventeen to go to Louisville, Kentucky, for college.

We moved to a farm when I was five years old. My dad began raising hogs, supplying many of the ethnic community "homes" (gathering places) with hogs for the Christmas and New Year's feasts. I almost hated those holidays. Even as children, we helped with the butchering of sometimes fifteen to twenty choates (pigs thirty-five to sixty pounds) that were delivered to the community homes.

My Adopted Grandfather

One person who played a significant role in my early life was Rev. Samuel DeLane, who adopted my father as a teenager after leaving Cheraw, South Carolina, because of a racial incident. DeLane also pastored the church I attended and baptized me at age five. I vividly remember going to him following Sunday school and telling him I wanted to be baptized. He called my dad over. After they both questioned me extensively, DeLane baptized me in June 1941.

When I was born, DeLane had insisted on the biblical eighth-day dedication. At that ceremony, DeLane named me, choosing a biblical name and predicting that I would preach. I did not know this until after I had preached my initial sermon on November 5, 1950. DeLane was no longer the pastor, having been displaced by the annual call. Reverend Frank Waller had replaced DeLane. DeLane asked for permission to make a statement after the sermon. In the statement he had eight people stand as witnesses. At that time he revealed his prediction that I would preach and that he had given me my name, Emmanuel Lemuel. The witnesses were sworn to secrecy and did not reveal any of this to me.

Reverend Frank Waller

Though DeLane served as a prominent figure in my life, Frank Waller made even more of an impact. Waller had always wanted a son "to give back to the Lord," but he was blessed with five daughters (though he gave boys' names to his last two daughters, Frankie Elizabeth and Charles Sydney). When I announced my sense of call to ministry at age fourteen, he lavished on me the attention a proud father would give a son. Instead of having me finish high school before beginning to preach, his philosophy was "learn by doing," in keeping with the Baptist Young People's Union (a church training organization that met on Sunday evenings) philosophy.

Even before I preached my initial sermon, Waller began taking me to associational meetings and sick visitations. I also assisted him in leading worship. He especially wanted me to be at funerals, performing any task that necessitated being near the body.

It was a long time before I discovered that Waller was afraid of the dead. My discovery of that fear came when I returned for a college break and went by to see him. A call came that a member had just passed. He said, "Come on. Let's go over to see about this widow." When we walked into the house he noted someone lying on the couch covered with a blanket. He walked over to remove it, asking, "Who's sleeping at a time like this?" The widow said, "That's him, Reverend." "Him who?" he responded. "My husband," she replied. Reverend Waller had assumed her husband had died at the hospital. He immediately went limp with fear. I had to help him to the car.

The three years of mentoring by Reverend Waller laid the foundation for my life and ministry. The values he taught me are still an intricate part of my life. I am the better for it.

Reverend Waller also introduced me to friends of his when we went to conventions and other religious meetings. These people helped me when I went to Louisville. They were concerned about my welfare. Fortunately there was never a crisis, but one of his close friends did invite me to assist him at his church.

Chapter 2

The Louisville Years

I would not want anyone to think that the part of Pennsylvania I grew up in was totally free of color prejudice. If it was present; however, I was not aware of it.

My pastor, Reverend Waller, wanted my cousin, Albert Preston, and me to go to the school he attended for ministerial training. Simmons University had at one time been a full-fledged university, but in the 1930s had lost its status. The General Association of Baptists in Kentucky did retain the theological department and the name. With great send-off, Valley Baptist Church, Wheatland, Pennsylvania, sent two of its sons off to college in fall 1953.

My first real confrontation with racial prejudice came when I changed trains from the B&O (Baltimore & Ohio) line to the L&N (Louisville & Nashville) line in Cincinnati. I noticed the conductor directing African Americans to one train and whites to another. I really knew I had arrived in a segregated society when I disembarked in Louisville. My cousin and I attempted to get a cab to campus. We were told abruptly to go to the "N" cab. Later, we went into a hamburger shop and sat at the counter; only to have the patrons at the counter move to the other end. No one spoke to us, but wickedly stared. Suddenly the warnings we had been given about how to conduct ourselves in a segregated society took on life. From then on the lessons came regularly as other students and members of the church we attended shared their experiences and wisdom.

Simmons Bible College.

Although Simmons was a disappointment, neither of us was in a financial position to do anything different. Our parents could not put us in other colleges. We knew we would have to work our way through. Louisville offered us an opportunity to do that since more jobs and colleges were available.

On our first day of class we met Dr. Garland K. Offutt. Offutt was the first African American to graduate from The Southern Baptist Theological Seminary in 1946. During the years of his study he was prevented from sitting in class with the other students because of the Day Law, which prohibited the mixing of races. The administration accommodated him by placing a chair in the hall outside the class so he could listen through the door. He took some classes in his professors' offices. Offutt did this for both the M.Th. and Th.D. programs. In 1950, the Day Law was voided by the Kentucky legislature, making it possible for anyone to attend classes anywhere in Kentucky's colleges and universities.

Offutt was careful to help us understand that Simmons was designed for men who entered the ministry late in life and had no other options for training. Both of us were young enough to go on to a full college program and then prepare for seminary. Because we had no other financial support, Al and I remained at Simmons for the first year and then transferred to the University of Louisville in fall 1954.

In 1954, representatives from several schools and seminaries organized a student-led movement, the South-wide Conference for Racial Reconciliation. Dr. Victor Glass, then academic dean at the American Baptist College, Nashville, was one of the leading spirits, along with Dr. Henlee Barnette (Southern Baptist Seminary), Rev. Joseph Conley (Baptist Fellowship Center, Louisville), and Dr. T. B. Maston (Southwestern Baptist Seminary, Fort Worth). This three-day meeting was significant because it was organized by Southern Baptists. The participating schools included American Baptist College, Simmons Bible College, Southern and Southwestern Baptist Seminaries, Berea College, and Fisk University. This was my first exposure to an organized attempt at racial reconciliation. I also got to meet men who would play significant roles later in my life.

1954–1958: The University of Louisville Years.

Enrolling into college was an all-day, table-hopping process. The requirements were not consolidated. One of the tables was the "religious preference table." I signed up for "Baptist," and my card was given to the Baptist Student Union (BSU).

Two days later, the director of the BSU and two students showed up at my door. They invited me to come to the BSU Center and informed me of the various activities. I immediately went with them. From then on, the BSU became my family.

With the BSU local and statewide activities, I became a first. In most instances, no other blacks were involved. When I was elected to the BSU Council, word reached the Long Run Baptist Association, the local sponsor for the BSU, that blacks, Asians, and Indians were BSU members. A committee came to tell the BSU that non-Southern Baptists could not attend or participate in any activities. This also meant that students from American Baptist churches across the river in Indiana could not participate either. The director, Fred Witty, and the other students were enraged. Following a two-hour discussion, for which I was present, the students gave the association an ultimatum: If the non-Anglo and American Baptist students could not participate, they would organize another student organization and boycott the Long Run-sponsored organization. A week later the response came back that any Baptist student could participate in the BSU. The victory was not without its consequences. Fred Witty was forced to seek a more congenial place of service. He went to Johnson City, Tennessee, where he served with distinction until retirement.

My college years were also a time of developing my place in denominational service. I joined the Green Street Baptist Church upon my arrival in 1953. The acting president of Simmons Bible College, Dr. Jesse Bottoms, was its pastor and a very gracious man who extended a warm welcome to my cousin and me.

In January 1954, one of Reverend Waller's friends called to ask if I was available to assist him. Reverend Arvel Carroll pastored the Joshua Tabernacle Baptist Church in Louisville. He had a growing congregation, including a large number of youth, and he needed someone to help him with youth emphases. He did not offer a salary, but he did agree to let me preach one Sunday a month, for which I would receive a love offering. I wanted the experience and challenge and began immediately.

Most of the people at Joshua Tabernacle Baptist Church had menial jobs (maids, cooks, housekeepers, yardmen, construction, custodial), but that did not prohibit their generosity. As a college student, I was a symbol of their hopes and aspirations. They were very generous not only in their love offerings, but from time to time some would put pieces of money in a handshake. I grew much during those years. I made mistakes for which they were patient and encouraging. I learned from my mistakes and am better for the experience.

It was also at Joshua Tabernacle that I met Emma Marie Johnson, one of the pianists for the church. We formed an attachment that later led to engagement and marriage. Marie came from a dedicated family that included an older sister and two younger brothers. During our courtship I was accepted into their family, including Sunday dinners. As a student working my way through college, there was little money for a proper date. Our weekly date amounted to walking home from church on Sunday evenings. The nine-block walk gave us additional time together. As the saying goes, "I married beyond myself." Marie has been a genuine companion, an ideal preacher's wife, a mother to our children, and a continual support as I have been busy with religious work. Her secretarial skills are par-excellent and have benefited my ministry greatly.

An Introduction into Denominational Life.

In 1956, I was asked to become a college intern with the Long Run Baptist Association. Long Run was in partnership with the Central District Baptist Association (black) in a ministry center, which also became the place where associational projects were housed. I was assigned to develop the Royal Ambassadors program for the Central District. At that time, the Royal Ambassadors were under the direction of the Woman's Missionary Union. The internship was paid by the Home Mission Board. I gave about fifteen hours a week working with the Central District churches, helping to develop Royal Ambassadors chapters and assisting with the programs of the Fellowship Center.

In 1957, the Woman's Missionary Union published the Home Mission Study for the Annie Armstrong Week of Prayer. The book, *The Long Bridge*, looked at the interracial ministry of Dr. Guy Bellamy of Oklahoma. Bellamy, who once served as Director of Intercity Missions for Oklahoma City, succeeded in helping Anglos, Native Americans, Hispanics, and African Americans work across racial lines in various aspects of church-related ministries. He was added to the staff of the Home Mission Board in 1955 to help Southern Baptists do the same thing. In 1957, Dr. Victor Glass was added to the Atlanta staff to do the administrative work. Bellamy was more of a PR person. He was permitted to live and work from Oklahoma City since he refused to fly and could get around adequately by train.

The study book was opposed by the SBC Executive Committee. The organized activity of the Civil Rights movement was beginning, and the SBC opposed the book's emphasis on racial reconciliation. They insisted that the book be taken out of the bookstores. While the Woman's Missionary Union was obedient, they were not submissive. There were other ways to get the book out. A later vignette will show how they distributed and promoted the study.

I was aware of these events as a student intern. I decided it was worth keeping the copy that I got. But I also began noticing other news articles, books, and media pieces related to the SBC and race. This prompted me to keep everything of use that I could.

The Southern Baptist Theological Seminary

It was understood that I would attend The Southern Baptist Theological Seminary when I finished the University of

Louisville. I entered in January 1959 when Southern was still recuperating from the loss of thirteen faculty who left in 1957.

Some of my introductory courses were taught by graduate students who later went on to become outstanding in their areas. I mention particularly William Hull (New Testament), Pierce Matheney (Old Testament), Ronald Deering (Greek), and B. A. Sizemore (Hebrew) because they continued their doctoral study while teaching us.

The one class I remember above all the rest is Hebrew. Sizemore weighted the final grade toward our ability to translate and dissect Jeremiah 30:30–33. Had the final test been given a week before exam week or two weeks afterward, I would have aced it. Unfortunately, during the week of exams, I was running between lawyers and court dockets. The little church I was serving, the Twenty-Eighth Street Baptist Church, was being sued by the former pastor. Members had returned to the church after being driven out. We were beginning to see an increase in energy and enthusiasm. The former pastor sued for unpaid salary. I had never been in court. I was embarrassed, unfamiliar, and scared of all that was happening. My personal anger toward the former pastor also affected my attitude and judgment.

When I went into the Hebrew exam, my mind went blank. I received the only "F" in my entire academic experience. There was a legend that the curbstones around the seminary drives, the "Hebrew Stones," were memorials to those who flunked Hebrew. One was named for me. I repeated the course the next fall under the guidance of Dr. Page Kelly, who had been brought back from the seminary in Brazil. He understood my plight. I still had to repeat the class, but he gave me translation assignments. I sat in the back of the class doing those while the rest of the class was conducted. Consequently,

I fell in love with Hebrew and went on to take other electives in Old Testament studies.

The years 1959–1963 affected Southern Seminary in interesting ways. All of us were affected by the national crises in the Civil Rights movement. Some students brought their homegrown hostilities and attitudes with them. They were challenged by a faculty that was committed to taking the "high road." Professors taught biblical principles of Christian ethics and behavior. Some participated in various Civil Rights actions and initiatives. I don't recall ever hearing of a faculty member who exhibited an unchristian attitude toward race or who defended the status quo. In 1956, the faculty took a unanimous stand against the Baptist Hospital for denying service to the wife of a Nigerian student, Theophilus Adagemobe. They later stood together and invited Adagemobe to teach introductory New Testament. They were equally adamant about the churches in the area being open to all students.

At the time, the majority of students of color were African or Caribbean. There were seldom more than two American blacks on campus at any given time. Marie and I were treated respectfully. We lived on campus in Rice Hall and later Judson. The students always had barbecues or croquette games on the open areas around Levering Gymnasium or on the Josephus Bowl to which we were invited. The women on each stairwell had Thursday night Woman's Missionary Union meetings that did much to bond them. Despite a few "hate stares," a common ploy of intimidation that lasted a short while, we had a wonderful social experience on Southern Seminary's campus.

I recall several times of fun when racial identity caused surprise. In 1960, the SBC met in Louisville. A special service was held in Alumni Chapel in dedication of the new library. Dr. Charles McGlon, the drama professor, wrote a play, *What*

Means These Stones. Done in the format of Greek theatre, student participants sat on stage in costumes representing their lines. I was one of the bricks. A cardboard box resembling a brick covered my head. At the end of the play we were asked to remove our masks and other headgear to be introduced to the audience. Some didn't know how to respond when I removed my brick.

My student years coincided with the presidency of Dr. Duke K. McCall. We often got our mail and telephone calls crossed due to having the same name. The president had a sense of humor and taught me how to have fun with it. I will relate a few of those instances.

Guess who Came to Church

An old historic church in east Jefferson County was having its 100th anniversary. The church was without a pastor at the time, so someone on the program committee called the Baptist Fellowship Center where I was interning and asked Rev. McCall to speak at the Wednesday night service. I agreed. At the time I didn't know they really wanted Dr. Duke McCall. They didn't know the difference between the Baptist Fellowship Center and The Southern Baptist Seminary. I was often asked to talk about the work of the Baptist Fellowship Center at Anglo churches in the area, so the invitation seemed natural.

I arrived on the appointed night at this semi-rural setting. The crowd was gathered out front waiting to go in. When I got out of the car, I was asked if I was Dr. McCall's chauffeur. I replied, "No. I am your speaker for tonight." Suddenly there was confusion all around. One brother came over to warn me that if I was looking for trouble, he would surely give it to me. (This was the era of kneel-ins and pray-ins, a part of the Civil

Rights strategies.) I assured him and the others that I was not looking for trouble. I was a student at The Southern Baptist Seminary and an intern at the Baptist Fellowship Center, and a call had come from that church inviting me to come. As I started to leave, another brother came over, apologized, and said to the others, "I want to hear what he has to say. We ain't got no other preacher for tonight." I went in. The service was strained. I remembered Duke McCall's humor. Before long, they were laughing. Eventually, they relaxed and accepted me. It turned out to be a good service. The next time I went to that church, they wanted Emmanuel, not Duke.

The Fantasy BWA Trip. In 1965 the Baptist World Alliance Congress met in Miami. I had finished seminary and was living in the Twenty-Eighth Street Baptist Church parsonage. Two weeks before the Baptist World Alliance met, I was reading the morning paper and noted that a classmate of mine had received an anonymous gift to attend the Baptist World Alliance. Privately, I was wishing that it could happen to me. The phone rang. The voice on the other end started right off: "Dr. McCall, this is your travel agent. I am calling to confirm your trip to Miami. Your flight number is _____, leaving on _____. You are using a Hertz rental car _____. Your hotel is _____ , located at _____. Now one piece of information I need is to know when you plan to leave Miami for _____. You are to preach at the First Baptist Church at _____. " It was then that the bubble burst. I knew she had the wrong McCall. I doubt that I could have been the janitor in the church she named.

Mistaken Identity. By 1972 I had been at the Home Mission Board for four years. I was invited back to a student missions conference at Southern. The weekend began with a Friday evening banquet. Dr. Duke McCall was the speaker.

We were sitting together. The student chairman spoke long and glowingly of President McCall and the contributions he had made. It got to be embarrassing. Duke leaned over and said, "Emmanuel, when he gets finished, you get up and go to the podium." I did. At first there was total confusion. Then, there was a burst of laughter. The humor saved the moment.

President McCall and I did that same thing the next spring at the SBC Executive Meeting. Duke was sitting at his assigned desk. I was back in the galley. Whoever was presenting him waxed eloquently to the point of being ridiculous. Knowing that I was in the hall, Duke swiveled around in his chair and caught my eye. I knew what to do next. At the appropriate time I made the long walk down the aisle. Those who didn't know me were unduly perplexed. Those who knew me howled with laughter.

My seminary years and the spin-offs of those experiences were great times. In 1971, I was invited to teach a J term class in a new effort encouraged by Drs. Henlee Barnette and Morgan Patterson. Beginning around 1965, Barnette had invited me often to speak in his ethics classes about racial matters. When I was taking Baptist history with Dr. Patterson, I did a paper on the history and development of black Baptists. Up until that time little had been written about the subject. Dr. Patterson was impressed enough with my research that I was often invited to lecture in his classes.

In 1970, following lectures in both of their classes, the idea was raised about a continuing emphasis on black church studies. I was invited to begin doing a class in January 1971. This action is referenced in Dr. Henlee Barnette's memoir, *A*

Pilgrimage of Faith.[1] The popularity of the class and the need to explore other areas of the black church led to an expanded program. Courses in black church history, the black church and social justice, the hermeneutics of the black church, and the general course, the black church, were offered in each of the three J terms. I taught one of them and recommended those who would teach the others. We had such distinguished men as Drs. J. DeOtis Roberts, Thomas Kilgore, George Kelsey, Edward Wheeler, Carlisle Driggers, Otis Moss Jr., J. Alfred Smith, Gayraud Wilmore, James Melvin Washington, Wendel Whalum, Benjamin Baker, W. J. Hodge, Mack King Carter, Dearing King, and Wilbert Goatley Sr. among the faculty. My last class was in 1996. I continue to meet former students who express appreciation for how the program prepared them to minister holistically.

At the request of the SBC Seminary Presidents Retreat, I spent an evening sharing with them the program. Dr. Roy Honeycutt initiated the invitation. Three of the SBC seminaries later adapted the program for their use.

National Alumni President

I also had the joy of serving on the National Alumni Council from 1991–1993. I was president in 1992, during which time we had a celebration at the campus before going to Indianapolis for the SBC and one of the largest alumni gatherings in our history. Some 1,800 persons attended the luncheon.

---

[1] Henlee Barnette, *A Pilgrimage of Faith: My Story* (Macon GA: Mercer University Press, 2004) 119.

I also received from Southern Seminary its most prestigious honorary recognition, the E. Y. Mullins Award for Distinguished Denominational Service, in 1990.

Chapter 3

Southern Baptist
Denominational Life

I am making a conscious distinction here because I participated in denominational life with the National Baptist Convention, Inc., and the Progressive National Baptist Convention prior to my activity in Southern Baptist life. I had the joy of serving as the National Youth Leader for the Progressive Baptist Congress in its organizational efforts of 1963. I was in that capacity for a four-year term.

My full participation in SBC life began in 1968. In 1967 Dr. Arthur Rutledge and the Home Mission Board made a decision to bring an African American on staff for the following reasons: (1) to help Southern Baptists understand and respond positively to the problem of racism, (2) to help Southern Baptists learn how to relate cooperatively with National Baptists, and (3) to help Southern Baptist churches that wished to be inclusive in membership.

Dr. Hugo Culpepper, who had been my missions professor at Southern, served a five-year span at the Home Mission Board as Director of Missions. He was aware of my ministry in racial reconciliation efforts in Louisville. He mentioned me to Dr. Victor Glass, director of the Department of Work with National Baptists. Reverend Cecil Ethredge,

Missionary Personnel Department, did an initial interview on his recruiting visit to Southern Seminary. He gave his recommendation to the chain of command. After a week of conversation with Dr. Glass and his associate, Dr. Wendell Grigg, and further talk with Dr. Culpepper, I was then presented to Dr. Arthur Rutledge and his associate, Dr. Fred Mosely. A final recommendation was made to the Executive Committee of the Home Mission Board's Board of Directors and then to the full board.

Everyone was aware of the potential for negative response to the Home Mission Board. This would be the first time an African American would be brought to the staff of any SBC agency. The volatility of the times could trigger a negative response that would affect the work of the Home Mission Board. Care was taken to be sure everything was done "above board," while also avoiding emotional flare-ups from others.

On May 9, 1968, my election was official. The national media picked it up. The headlines read, "Southern Baptists Elect a Negro Executive." I received many congratulatory notes from former classmates, seminary professors, pastors, and laypeople. I am sure there was opposition to my election, but I never received those notes. I inquired from the Home Mission Board news service about negative responses, but none were reported. Perhaps I was shielded from them. I remembered the subscription cancellations that came to the Home Mission magazine for placing the picture of Dr. William Holmes Borders on the front cover of the January 1967 issue. I still have copies of the letters from the eight Southern Baptist churches in the Atlanta area that welcomed and invited us to join their church.

A Shift in Emphasis

As the reader can now see, I am beginning to talk more about the need for racial reconciliation in the SBC, and the focus of my ministry. For this reason I need to lay a foundation. The reader needs to know how racism in the South began, developed, was promoted, and how it became so much a part of SBC life. I will shift thought to the purely historical, and then continue narratives of memoir. Some of these narratives will be vignettes, glimpses through special experiences. Others will be fuller descriptions of how God was at work changing the minds of Baptists in the South.

A Glimpse at the Past. An attempt to look at the progress in racial attitudes among Southern Baptists from 1957–1995 is futile without understanding how racial perspectives developed. A brief history mentioning the salient factors is necessary.

Initial Explorations. When explorers from Europe came in contact with the Americas they found new opportunities for expansion of their colonialism, domination of territories, and accumulation of wealth. Those from Holland, Portugal, England, France, and Spain found an abundance of natural resources such as rice, cotton, corn, tobacco, and cane sugar in North and South America and the Caribbean Islands. To obtain this wealth, fields had to be cleared and more land placed under cultivation. The questions raised were, "Where would the human resources be found? How could this wealth be harvested at minimum cost?"

History verifies that America's South was settled by a combination of adventurers, those wanting to escape persecutions, some wanting a new life in the new land, some set free from prisons, others sent as emissaries, indentured servants, and contract settlers. Other kinds of persons were needed to maximize the opportunities for profit. Human slavery provided an easy option. Slaves could be secured from African tribal wars, brought to the Americas, and used to provide cheap labor. This was the beginning of the three-way slave trade passage.

The Outward Passage. The manifests of ships involved in the slave trade indicate that ships left Europe with cloth, beads, rum, guns, and other metal-ware, sailing to Africa's west coast to territories now known as Senegal, Gambia, Guinea, Ghana, Liberia, and Nigeria. This cargo was exchanged for "human cargo"—that is, slaves. The slaves were captives of tribal wars and sold by African chieftains to the Europeans. Consequently, whole tribes were decimated by their greed.

The Middle Passage. The Middle Passage brought these captives in "slave holds" of ships from Africa to North and South America and the Caribbean Islands. All who left Africa did not reach the destination. Some died of disease or were killed en route. The patterns of slave trade were the same in the Western Hemisphere: cultural confusion, docilizing, disorientation, and re-orientation. The methods used by Nebuchadnezzar of Babylon (Daniel 1) were repeated with African slaves: (1) Put some in charge of their fellows; (2) change their names (cultural and religious re-orientation); (3) change their diet and relationships (social re-orientation); (4) change their religious practices.

The Homeward Passage. The Homeward Passage exchanged human cargo for the commodities of the New World—rum, tobacco, rice, corn, sugar, and cotton to take back to Europe.

Attempts at Justification. How does one justify the conditions related to slavery? Various attempts were made. Europeans and white Americans developed racial superiority theories. Particular notice was given to the darkness of the skin of the enslaved. Writers, like William Shakespeare, seized upon the opportunity to profit from this notion. Shakespeare emphasized the "whiteness" of Queen Elizabeth's breast in contrast to the darkness of his own black mistress in order to secure the queen's patronage for his theatre.[2]

The fact that Africans wore few clothes was used to portend animal-like sub-humanness. No thought was given to the fact of extreme heat and the negative effects of cloth materials.

Additionally, attention was called to the shape of the Africans' heads. Cranial theories began and were amplified to justify and excuse slavery. These theories posited inferior mind based upon the size and shape of the skull.

Sailors, merchants, and traders, who were neither sociologists, medical scientists, nor psychologists, made other generalizations. These generalizations were passed on as authentic and factual. Biblical and theological gymnastics appeared to give divine sanction to slavery. Some acted as though they were doing the Africans a favor by bringing them from a "heathen" land to a "civilized" existence.

One of the chapters will deal with the "Curse of Ham" myth, which was promoted as a biblical basis for human slavery. Tragically, it was believed to be the "inspired" word of God by many until the scholarship of the 1960s refuted it. Some still believe and teach such fallacious interpretations.

Selected passages from the New Testament, especially the letters of the Apostle Paul, were used to justify slavery and to keep slaves under subjection. Philemon, 1 Corinthians 7:20–21,

---

[2] Winthrop Jordan, *White Over Black: American Attitudes Toward the Negro, 1550–1812* (Chapel Hill: University of North Carolina Press, 1968) 8.

Ephesians 6:5–9, Colossians 3:22–4:1, 1 Timothy 6:20–21 were all proof-texts to suggest biblical justification for slavery.

Some prominent Southern Baptist leaders, such as Richard Fuller of South Carolina, became staunch defenders of the slave system, even owning slaves: "What God sanctioned in the Old Testament, and permitted in the New, cannot be sin."[3]

Walter Shurden[4] describes slavery as "the cultural earthquake that shook the nation between 1830 and 1865." Southern Baptists organized in defense of slavery and in support of "Southern Culture." The Baptist voice against slavery was most often silent. Only a few occasionally spoke loud enough to be heard. As Baptist associations encountered local hostility for any opposition to slavery, they backed off.

God Works in Mysterious Ways. Baptists are fond of saying that "God works in mysterious ways." When England's Society for the Propagation of the Gospel (SPG) began printing pamphlets against slavery in 1701 and its missionary successor, the Society for the Propagation of the Gospel in Foreign Parts, began sending missionaries to evangelize the slaves, religion entered the controversy in a new way. The question was raised as to whether or not the slave had a soul and the capacity for being saved. The debate was extensive. The sentiment was that the slave had an inferior soul, and thus could be retained as a slave. An English slave code said if it could be proven that the enslaved had a soul, then freedom had to be granted.[5]

---

[3] H. Shelton Smith, *In His Image, But...: Racism in Southern Religion, 1780–1910* (Durham NC: Duke University Press, 1972).

[4] Walter B. Shurden, *Not a Silent People* (Nashville TN: Broadman Press, 1972) 52.

[5] Jordan, *White Over Black*, 49–52.

The question of "religious capacity" was also posed. Capacity related to the intellectual ability to understand Anglo religious practices and styles. To imply equal religious capacity logically implied equal intellectual capacity. Of course, denied the opportunity for literate skills, the slaves could not be expected to use prayer books, follow liturgies, or express theology as whites did. Otis Moss is helpful at this point: "Suppose Fred Shuttlesworth, Ralph Abernathy, and Martin Luther King, Jr., facing Bull Connor in Birmingham, had pulled out a prayer book, reading in Latin, and then called upon a European-styled choir director to lead the group singing 'A Mighty Fortress Is Our God.' All the water hoses of Bull Connor would have washed the whole freedom movement down the very streets of history. The angels would have cried, and the devils would have giggled with glee."[6]

One of the "mysterious ways" through which God worked was the "Great Awakenings," spiritual revivals that began in England and were continued in America by men like Jonathan Edwards, John and Charles Wesley, George Whitfield, and Samuel Davies. The spiritual revival in America began in New England and moved down the coast. It took a special life of its own when it reached the South (Virginia) and the western frontier (Ohio). The spiritual peaks occurred between 1750–1790, 1790–1830, and 1830–1860.[7] They were developed in outdoor activities that continued for weeks and months at a time. Phenomena such as spirited preaching, singing, creating new music, barking like dogs, shouting, jerking, rolling on the

---

[6] Emmanuel McCall, *Black Church Lifestyles* (Nashville TN: Broadman Press, 1986) 18.

[7] Eugene Genovese, *Roll, Jordan, Roll* (New York: Vintage Press, 1974) 184.

ground, and holy laughing were expressed in these services. People were brought to salvation and a new way of living. Some acknowledged "the call to preach" even though they lacked basic and formal literate skills. They had a testimony that they told with unbridled enthusiasm. This began new perspectives on the ministry and the task of preaching.

Attending to the needs of their masters were the slaves. They "kept house" for the tent dwellers, prepared foods, and did other necessary chores. The slaves were in the environment and were caught up in the same phenomena of their masters. Everything they did, the slaves did also. The debate on whether or not the slaves had souls was replaced with this reality: "Since they do have souls, what happens next?"

The "what next" was that three distinct patterns of religious practices developed among the slave population. For instance, some masters allowed the slaves to worship with them in their churches. Some sat in the same "pews" (family section). Other churches had special places such as a slave section or balcony. There is an architectural theory that balconies developed as a place to put slaves.

A second option was that church houses were built for slaves. On Sunday afternoons, after the white preacher finished dinner, he would go to the slave church for worship. As slave preachers began to be acknowledged, some were used as "exhorters." They either interpreted what the white preacher was saying or prepared the crowd for the preacher. One recalls the old *Sanford & Son* TV shows where the white policeman always needed "Smitty," the black policeman, to tell Fred Sanford what was being said.

Even as whites received the "call" to preach out of those protracted meetings, so did the slaves. Slave preachers became a concern for the system. They freely applied freedom in

Christ to freedom from bondage. The great slave revolts were led by slave preachers—Gabriel Prosser (Virginia, 1800) Denmark Vessey (South Carolina, 1821), and Nat Turner (Virginia, 1831). For that reason, slave preachers were seldom allowed to conduct services without supervision.

The third option for slave worship was the "Brush Harbor" services, also referred to as "Hush Harbor" meetings. These were most often held at night, down in the woods or some other isolated place, under a "lean to" of poles covered with brush to deaden the sound. For slaves on plantations, where the exercise of religion was forbidden, or for slaves who did not want the "big house" to know what was going on, those secret places became their places of refuge.

The late Dearing E. King of Louisville, Kentucky, and Chicago, Illinois, often repeated his grandmother, who told how a field slave might lead in singing "Steal Away" constantly as the others were at their chores: "Steal away, steal away, steal away to Jesus; / Steal away, steal away home; I ain't got long to stay here." She said this was a code telling other slaves there would be a meeting that night in the woods.

Sometimes the enthusiasm in worship was loud. If the "big house" heard the worshipers, they could be punished or killed. To give a sense of relief the next morning, a house slave might venture near field slaves singing, "I couldn't hear nobody pray, I couldn't hear nobody pray; / 'Way down yonder by myself and I couldn't hear nobody pray." The interpretation of the code was, "You were not heard at the 'big house.'"

African Americans, both slave and free, responded overwhelmingly to the religious expressions that flavored the Great Awakenings in the South. Those expressions were attractive because of the appeal to emotion and the creative freedom for emotional response. One could fashion the whole worship experience—songs, sermons, and prayers—to one's situation in life. By comparison, the Baptist expression allowed that freedom to blossom. Other denominations had their traditions and liturgies, which were both confining and defining. As Otis Moss[8] says,

> In the highly sophisticated, liturgical church, everything was organized years before they got to that moment: the order of worship—the prayers and hour of worship or the experience of worship. The prayers were all written out in the book. The slaves could not carry a prayer book around in their hip pockets out in the cotton fields, in order to say: "Lord, bless the Queen of England and all of her cabinet. Bless the government and the Parliament." They didn't have the time to go through all of that. In fact, they were unable to read.
>
> But as the sun made its journey, or as the earth made its revolution, they looked toward the setting of the sun and said:
>
> "This evening, our Heavenly Father, it's once more and again that this, your humble servant, knee bent and body bowed, one more time. And as I bow, I want to thank you for my last night's lying down. I want to thank you for a guardian angel that you sent to watch over me all night long while I slumbered and slept. I want to thank you because you touched me with a finger of love this morning, and woke me up in due time. I yet have the activity of my limbs, and my tongue

---

[8] McCall, *Black Church Lifestyles*, 13.

was not cleaved to the roof of my mouth. I was yet left in a gospel and Bible-reading country."

Then they looked around at a mean boss man and said: "where mens and womens won't do right."[9]

Slaves and free African Americans responded to the Baptist church in large numbers. Until the Civil War, there were more black Southern Baptists than Anglo.[10] This is explained by the fact that the number of slaves exceeded the members of the ruling family. Slave membership privileges were often restricted. Most were illiterate by their master's designs.

In his book *Religion on the American Frontier: The Baptists*, William Warren Sweet includes the records of the business meetings of ten churches in Kentucky. One is particularly struck by those of the Forks of the Elkhorn Baptist Church, 1800–1820, which include statements of admission to the church; requests for letters of dismissal; and "churchings," in which members were brought before the church charged for moral or spiritual offenses. Some were forgiven ("we will bear with him"), but others were dismissed.

Pertinent to this discussion are the records relating to black members, both slave and free. I have selected representative statements:

---

[9] Ibid.

[10] Arthur B. Rutledge, *Mission to America: A Century and a Quarter of Southern Baptist Home Missions* (Nashville TN: Broadman Press, 1969) 129.

Recd by Experience Condorces Belonging to Jas Saunders (received by Christian experience Condorces, a slave belonging to James Saunders)[11]

Saturday Evening the Church met and after Divine Worship proceeded to business and recd. By Experience Robert Hickling; John Brown Jr a Black woman belonging to Bro. Wm. Brown Named Sarah Samuel, Gravat, James a Black man belonging to Geo Madison[12]

The 2nd Saturday in January 1807 after divine Worship proceeded to business. Complaint brought against Sister Esther Boulwares Winney 1st for saying she once thought it her duty to serve her Master and Mistress but since the Lord had converted her, she had never believed that any Christian kept Negroes or Slaves[13]

Bro. Palmer brought a complaint against Bro. Stephens and Wife for not leeting Nancy (a slave) come to see her Child—Referd to next meeting[14]

Sunday after Sermon the Church set and Excluded Joe the property of Mr. Geo. Carlisle and Charity the

---

[11] William W. Sweet, *Religion on the American Frontier: The Baptists* (New York: Cooper Square Publishers, 1964) 274.

[12] Ibid., 281.

[13] Ibid., 328–29.

[14] Ibid., 323.

property of Mr. Francis Peartwho was Man and Wife, for frequently Quarreling and Parting.[15]

Joe the Property of Samuel Moxleys, Decdt is granted a letter of Dismission[16]

Anakey the property of Bro. John Price is Restored to fellowship in this church[17]

Agreable to an order of Our Last Church meating the Committey have Exammened the Church Book and find the amount of members as following: To Wit 25 White Males and 54 White fealmales and 47 Slaves and Persons of Culler the whole amounting to 126 members[18]

For saying she believed there was Thousands of white people Wallowing in Hell for their treatment to Negroes—and she did not care if there was as many more—Refer'd to next Meeting[19]

Freedom for some slave preachers was purchased so that they could be free to preach and pastor. The Maryland Baptist Union Association freed Rev. Noah Davis in 1849.[20] The Montgomery County Baptist Association in Alabama

---

[15] Ibid., 331.
[16] Ibid., 402.
[17] Ibid., 403.
[18] Ibid., 402.
[19] Ibid., 329.
[20] Rutledge, *Mission to America*, 129.

purchased freedom for Caesar McLemore in 1828.[21] The
Concord Association of United Baptists (Tennessee) freed
Edmund Kelley.[22]

There appear to be other exceptions to the generalizations
often made about this period of time. For all of the viciousness
of slavery, other humane things occurred, some of which will
be referenced in this book.

After the War

Following the Civil War, black and white Baptists parted ways.
White Baptists focused on recovery and reconstruction of their
way of life. In some instances their anger caused them to expel
the newly freed black members who began pressing for full
recognition. Other white congregations were decimated by the
eager departure of their black members.

Ed Wheeler[23] refers the departure of black church
members as "the Uplift of the Race." Blacks and whites had
different agendas. Blacks emphasized education, public
acceptance, trade skills, political and social recognition, and the
general well-being of their populations. This led black
churches to form their own associations, conventions,
fraternities, etc. They were aided by Baptists from the North
and previously freed blacks from the North and South.
Southern Baptists were caught in a psycho/spiritual bind. They
wanted to monitor and control the development of blacks in
the South, but they could not handle the goodwill of Northern

---

[21] Ibid.

[22] Ibid., 130.

[23] Edward Wheeler, *The Uplift of the Race: The Black Minister in the New
South: 1865–1902* (Lanham MD: University Press of America, 1986).

Baptists, who started educational centers for all levels of education for blacks.

After the war, racism blended with southern religion and culture in ways that completely alienated the races. There are only isolated instances of cooperation between black and white Baptists in the South between 1895 and 1920. The SBC's Home Mission Board sponsored institutes for training black ministers and assisted in some salaries for teacher missionaries, but beyond that little else happened.

In 1920 a new attempt at cooperation was initiated when the SBC and the National Baptist Convention, Inc., began the joint sponsorship of the American Baptist College in Nashville, Tennessee. They attempted to provide formal theological education for black ministers. The school still exists, though now it is solely sponsored by the National Baptist Convention, Inc.

A later initiative came with the appointment of Noble Y. Beall. Beall and his wife, Jewell, were committed to conscience-raising on behalf of all who were downtrodden or in need. This led them to include the black populations. Beall led an emphasis on Christian social ministries from the Home Mission Board. He was aided in 1942 by a consultant, Roland T. Smith. Smith helped J. B. Lawrence, General Secretary of the Home Mission Board, in decisions related to the black community. Technically speaking, Roland Smith was the first black to have an official staff role in the SBC. Unfortunately, it was only consultative. He held no authority, and his office was in his home.

The real changes began with the appointment of Guy Bellamy of Oklahoma as Secretary of Negro Work in 1949. The rest of the book tells the story.

Chapter 4

Brother Noah Was Drunk: Another Look at the Curse of Ham Myth

The Holy Bible has been misused by those who wish to validate their point of view. Having an idea and finding a Scripture to support the idea is an old and commonly used ploy. This ploy was used to justify slavery in America, providing a biblical safe haven for slave owners. Considering the historic position of Baptists in the South on biblical inerrancy, one sees how the misinterpretation of Scripture was used to justify a heinous sin.

An Analysis of the Tradition

I first heard of the notion that black people were made dark by a curse that God put upon Ham, one of the sons of Noah, when I was a child. Sincere Sunday school teachers in the little church where I grew up taught this idea, and preachers affirmed such nonsense. As recently as 1973, I heard the president of a National Baptist convention begin his address with these words: "The sons of Ham have gathered." Reverend P. B. Holley, a black man, was considered a scholar in his day. In his book *God and the Negro: Or the Biblical Record of the Race of Ham*, 1937, he expounded on and supported this thesis.

If this myth was considered true in black churches, one can only begin to imagine what was said in other groups. In the 1960s and 1970s, as Southern Baptists began having race relations conferences, the regularity of questions raised around this theme were astounding. For those who think that this notion is dead today, I only suggest you listen to some religious stations on AM radio or visit some churches outside or even in metropolitan centers.

The curse of Ham theory is not of American origin. According to H. Shelton Smith,[24] it was in circulation long before America was discovered. None of the sources indicate the specifics of the exact origin of the theory. We do know it was popularized and maximized during the period of American slavery. It was especially used in defense against abolitionists from about 1800–1865.

The tradition of the curse of Ham myth follows this general pattern: Following the flood, Noah planted a vineyard, which produced a bountiful harvest of grapes. With this harvest Noah made wine, which he later consumed until inebriated. While inebriated, Noah became unclothed. His son Ham, seeing Noah's nakedness, laughed in mockery instead of being embarrassed for him and covering his nakedness. Shem and Japheth, the other sons, hearing of their father's state, walked backward so as not to see his nakedness and covered him with a blanket. It was a sin for a child to see his father naked.

When Noah recovered and was told of Ham's deed, he supposedly placed a curse on Ham. The irreversible curse made the descendants of Ham servants to Shem and Japheth as

---

[24] H. Shelton Smith, *In His Image, But...: Racism in Southern Religion, 1780–1910* (Durham NC: Duke University Press, 1972) 131.

well as their descendants. Ham's descendants eventually settled in Africa from which the American slaves came. Therefore, slavery was ordained and sanctioned by God.

There are other variations and elaborations on this theme. Some saw African Slavery as punishment for wickedness. Others said the curse included Ham and his posterity. Somehow, "Ham" was interpreted to mean "black" of character and mind disposition. All of the worse of the human situation was folded into the word "black." For them skin color and evil character became synonymous. This became an accepted way of thinking.

A. H. Sayce attempts to attach colors to the names of Noah's sons. He says Japheth comes from the Assyrian "ippatu," meaning "white." Shem comes from the Assyrian "samu," meaning "olive colored." Ham comes from the Hebrew "khom," meaning "to be hot."[25]

J. C. Nott is responsible for the term "Niggerology," which he defined as the study of the origin of Negroes. In a letter dated February 14, 1849, he suggested five theories of the origin of "Negroes" based on the curse of Ham:[26]

(1) Negroes differentiated slowly from Noah.

(2) Ham was born black. God superintended the formation of two of the sons of Noah, in the womb of their mother, in an extraordinary and supernatural manner, giving to these children such forms of bodies,

---

[25] A. H. Sayce, *The Races of the Old Testament* (Oxford: The Religious Track Society, 1891) 41–42. Quoted in Everett Tilson, *Segregation and the Bible* (Nashville: Abingdon Press, 1958) 20.

[26] James Buswell, *Slavery, Segregation and Scripture* (Grand Rapids MI: William B. Eerdmans Publishing Company, 1964) 19–20.

constitutions of natures and complexions of skin as suited his will.... Japheth, he caused to be born white, while he caused Ham to be black, a color still further removed from the red hue of his parents than was white.[27]

(3) The races of men were transformed by God in the Tower of Babel episode. Here, races and languages were created and confounded together.

(4) The Negro constituted another species of man. Adam was father to only the white race.

(5) The Negro was a beast, not a human. He was in the ark, but he was not related to Noah. Ariel (a pseudonym for Buckner Payne) amplified this theory in "The Negro: What Is His Ethnological Status?" This tract, first written in 1840, was revised in 1867. He was one of several who attempted to make the Negro sub-human, akin to apes rather than man. This was indirectly related to one of the English slave codes, which allowed the enslavement if the species could be declared sub-human or non-human.

Josiah Clark Nott applied his inadequate knowledge of medical research by creating fictions of physiology. Nott was a South Carolinian who practiced medicine in Mobile, Alabama. Though lacking scientific ability, he achieved fame by publishing his cranial theories in 1844. According to Nott, Ham was "the gigantic negro" whose "form of body" included a vastly different skull, with bones made for stronger, thicker, harder, and more compact in relation to the sutures. The great

---

[27] Ibid., 19.

thickness was a "singular providence" for the Negro as it provided him with a powerful weapon, both of attack and defense.[28]

While Nott is not the originator of this physiological theorizing, he won acclaim by linking it to the curse of Ham. Winthrop Jordan,[29] in his chapter "Fruits of Passion," cites voluminous sources of the physiological "studies" occurring in the late 1600s, 1700s, and 1800s. Most of these were tied to the apologetics of interracial sex. The notions of black physical superiority were extended to the dimensions of sexual apparatus and emotion, thus leading Priest to say that not only does Ham mean "black" as a color of skin, but in a moral character that expresses itself in "beastly lusts and lasciviousness."[30]

Alexander McCaine delivered a speech before the General Conference of the Methodist Protestant Church in Baltimore in 1842. His speech was titled "Slavery Defended from Scripture, Against the Attacks of the Abolitionists." In this speech he says Noah "spoke under the impulse and dictation of Heaven. His words were the words of God himself, and by them slavery ordained. This was an early arrangement of God himself, to be perpetuated through all time."[31]

In an exchange of correspondence between the Rev. Richard Fuller of Beaufort, South Carolina, and the Rev. Francis Wayland, his abolitionist adversary from Providence, Rhode Island, Fuller titled one correspondence "Domestic

---

[28] Ibid., 20.

[29] Winthrop Jordan, *White Over Black: American Attitudes Toward The Negro, 1550–1812* (Chapel Hill: University of North Carolina Press, 1968).

[30] Buswell, *Slavery, Segregation and Scripture*, 17.

[31] Smith, *In His Image*, 130.

Slavery Considered as a Scriptural Institution" (1845). Basing his assumption on the accuracy of the curse of Ham myth, Fuller concluded that what God sanctioned in the Old Testament is permitted in the New Testament. Since the New Testament is silent on slavery (according to him), Jesus is on the side of the slaver owners.

The numerous references available indicate that this tradition was widely circulated, especially in the South, during the period of American slavery. While the rationale for the popularity of the tradition has diminished, the spirit of the tradition continues through the political rhetoric of welfare, busing, housing, etc.

An Evaluation of the Tradition

Everett Tilson[32] suggests seven false assumptions in the traditional interpretation of this passage of Scripture:

(1) That Shem, Ham, and Japheth are in fact the progenitors of distinct racial groups.
(2) That no further migration than that mentioned in Genesis 10 took place.
(3) That God pronounced the curse.
(4) That the curse was biologically transferable.
(5) That Ham was the original victim of the curse.
(6) That the original victim was Negroid.
(7) That the children of the original victims were to remain slaves.

Tilson offers the following in response to these false assumptions:

---

[32] Everett Tilson, *Segregation and the Bible* (Nashville TN: Abingdon Press, 1958) 20f.

(1) Noah, not God spoke the curse. God cannot be held responsible for the acts of a drunken man.

(2) History indicates that biblical curses are not always fulfilled. Some were. Others were not.

(3) The Bible emphatically states (Genesis 9:25) that the curse was upon Canaan, one of Ham's four sons. Therefore, only one-fourth of Ham's descendants had reason to regard themselves as affected by the curse.

(4) History has proven that the opposite of the curse has occurred. Canaan's descendants dominated Palestine for the first seventeen centuries.

(5) Egypt and Babylon (the descendants of Ham's sons, Mizraim and Nimrod) were pioneers in art, literature, and science, giving to us alphabetic writing, astronomy, history, agriculture, and the textile industry. Therefore, the curse could not have been on Ham and his sons.

Tilson concludes by affirming that either man misread God or that God was incapable of fulfilling the curse.

In an earlier paper[33] on this subject, I argued that in Noah's curse Noah was speaking for himself, not God. There are no other biblical instances where a man could use God's power to curse a whole people as a result of his own sinful conduct. Additionally, the Scripture is clear that Noah was woozy after his drunken stupor. He cursed his grandson, Canaan, not Ham, who had done the deed. There is no

---

[33] Emmanuel McCall, "Cursed Be Canaan—For What?," *Watchman Examiner* 7/3 (6 February 1969): 72–73.

indication that Canaan was anywhere near the scene. Yet what more could you expect of a drunk? (Further, I am amazed at the people who will fight the use of alcohol and are theoretically prohibitionists, but would hasten to this passage of Scripture to justify the enslavement and perpetual disrespect for other human beings.)

Since, according to the Scriptures, Noah did curse Canaan, and given that those supporting "Hamitic determinism" use this passage, it is interesting to note who the descendants of Canaan were: "And Canaan begat Sidon his firstborn, and Heth, and the Jebusite, and the Amorite, and the Girgasite, and the Hivite, and the Arkite, and the Sinite, and the Arvadite, and the Zemarite, and the Hamathite: and afterward were the families of the Canaanites spread abroad. And the border of the Canaanites were from Sidon, as thou comest to Gerar, unto Gaza: as thou goest, unto Sodom and Gomorrah, and Admah, and Zeboim even to Lasha."[34]

From this geographical description stated in the Bible, any person acquainted with biblical archeology can see that the boundaries of the Canaanites were the Bible lands of Palestine, not Africa. Sidon represents the northern boundary of Canaan; Gerar is the southwest boundary; Sodom, Gomorrah, Admah, and Zeboim were the four cities composing the southeast boundary. From what the Bible and biblical archeology tell us of the people that inhabited the area, they were Semites, people kindred to the Jews, not the blacks of Africa.

---

[34] Genesis 10:15–19 (KJV).

Let's Come Out of Noah's Stupor

The patterns of scriptural justification for slavery took a number forms.[35] These forms maintained from the first written defense of slavery in American history by John Saffin (1701) through the aftermath of the Emancipation Proclamation of 1863.

One such form was a general assertion that the institution of slavery was natural, ordained of God, a benefit to the enslaved. The "benefit" was supposedly in contrast to the myth of the African past and the "opportunities" in a "Christian" nation. The teachings regarding the Negroid race were based upon elaborations on the "Hamitic Curse."

Another form employed examples of slavery from the Old Testament and accepted their interpretations as "valid" because they were in the Bible. Similarly, it was often cited that instructions were given regarding the behavior of slaves toward their masters. These were moralized from the New Testament, especially Paul's letter to Philemon. Other instructional Scriptures included the obedience and subservience of slaves (Titus 2:9–10; Ephesians 6:5–9; Colossians 3:22–25; 1 Peter 2:18–25), regard for the master (1 Timothy 6:1–2; Ephesians 6:5–9), remaining in one's calling (1 Corinthians 7:20–24), and God's intended variety in human status (1 Corinthians 12:13–26).

These ideas regarding scriptural justifications for slavery were forms of "civil religion," a phrase used to describe the manipulation of religion and religious institutions for political, social, or economic ends. These "justifications" for slavery

---

[35] William W. Sweet, *Religion on the American Frontier: The Baptists* (New York: Cooper Square Publishers, 1964) 274.

were reapplied following the Civil War and used to validate the "reign of James Crow" (a euphemism for Jim Crow—the pattern of racial separation). They resurfaced again during the Civil Rights era of the 1960s. Their quick demise may be attributed to the rise of biblical principles of interpretation.

These ideas were engrained in Southern Baptists and had to be dealt with for racial reconciliation to occur. We are indebted to biblical interpreters, ethicists, practictioners of the faith, and people who loved the Lord for helping Southern Baptists confront racisim.

What Does the Contemporary Community of Faith Do with This Passage?

We do what most Southern Baptists have done with it in recent times: We consider it a sinful distortion of Scripture and correct it whenever it raises its ugly head; we apply the best of interpretive and hermeneutical principles to all of the word of God; and we continue to let the Holy Spirit empower us to be the presence of Christ in this sinful world.

Chapter 5

Understanding the Times

The years between 1957 and 1995 were filled with foment and change. Southern Baptists did not change attitudes about race out of a vacuum; rather, changing times led to changing racial attitudes.

Communities were in turmoil into the 1970s. The successful bus boycott in Baton Rouge, Louisiana, led by Rev. T. J. Jemison in 1953, became an instrument noted by blacks in other cities. *Brown v. Board of Education* was still being resisted and gerrymandered. Politicians like Orval Fabus and George Wallace galvanized racial resistance to the government's mandate. New hate groups came into being to aid the resistance. The turmoil begged for resolution.

The Montgomery Bus Boycott, which lasted from December 12, 1955, to December 21, 1956, inspired the need for a vehicle for confronting segregation. This led to the creation of the Southern Christian Leadership Conference (SCLC). Dr. Martin Luther King Jr. left Dexter Avenue Baptist Church in Montgomery, Alabama, to move to Atlanta, Georgia, where he would lead the SCLC. Concurrently, he became co-pastor with his father at Ebenezer Baptist Church. This began an era of demonstrations against all structures of society that were considered restrictive. Race was only one restriction. The feminist movement, the concern for special-needs persons, child abuse, Native Americans, migrant worker conditions, sweat shops, and workers' rights were only some of the concerns that were challenged. Because SCLC was religious, religious persons from all denominations and races joined the movement. A coalition of organizations joined forces under the general banner of civil rights.

A pivotal time in the Civil Rights Movement was the March on Washington, 1963, where King gave his famous "I Have a Dream" speech. The nation took his message seriously. In 1964 and 1965, Congress passed legislation declaring all public accommodations open regardless of race and giving voting rights to all citizens.

The various marches and demonstrations were followed by the news media and reported daily. Those in which force and brutality were involved had chilling effects as people watched the evening news. For example, the March 7, 1965, incident on the Edmund Pettis Bridge in Selma, Alabama, became known as "Bloody Sunday." The media reporting galvanized President Lyndon Johnson to press for the Voting Rights Act of 1965.

The South was exposed to the world in an embarrassing way. The consciences of Southern Baptists were also stirred. Prophetic voices among the SBC became more pronounced. College young people became activists. New communal groups emerged. "Flower children" and "hippies" left the campuses to crusade for their causes.

The year 1967 began a period of civil disorders. Grievances in urban areas resulted in mass rioting. Cities like Detroit, Cleveland, Newark, Chicago, and Los Angeles had communities that were destroyed. So serious was this period the president established a National Advisory Commission on Civil Disorders.

Reverend Billy Graham moved from a neutral position and began to use his influence for racial reconciliation. He insisted that every facet of his crusades be open to all people. He began using blacks in prominent ways on the platform. Because of his popularity among Southern Baptists, his influence was felt.

This period also saw the rise of black pride and a revival of interest in all things African. Afro hairstyles became popular, and the wearing of African clothing and jewelry was fashionable. Black scholars began traveling to Africa to research their heritage. Alex Haley's book *Roots* and the television series it spawned did much to help America understand the period of slavery, the injustices that accompanied it, and the origin of America's racial attitudes. It also caused the black community to become more intentional about rediscovering its histories.

Black community and church leaders formed their own organizations to address problems of the race: the National Committee of Negro Churchmen (NCNC), the Congress on Racial Equality (CORE), the Student Non-Violent Coordinating Committee (SNCC), the Inter-religious Foundation for Community Organization (IFCO), and the Black Economic Development Committee (BEDC). Blacks in majority-white denominations formed black caucuses whose purposes were to have those denominations address the concerns of the black community. "Black" replaced the word "Negro."

There were also "revolutionary" groups (groups advocating the use of violence to achieve black rights) that developed, such as the Black Panthers and Revolutionary Action Movement. The Nation of Islam, influenced by Louis Farrakhan, made statements that were intimidating to both blacks and whites. At that time they were more popularly known as "Black Muslims."

In a separate vignette I have referred to the "Black Manifesto" and its impact. This is just a glimpse of some of the things going on between 1957 and 1995. But what was happening among Southern Baptists?

A number of preachers stood courageously in their churches, communities, and denominational structures. They preached about equality, justice, the nature of godly love, brotherhood, and the kingdom of God. Some lost their pulpits, their teaching positions, their denominational positions. Some lost their voice in Southern Baptist circles. Some have scars in their souls. Some lost their families. Some left the ministry.

Another event that stirred Southern Baptists was the 1957 missions study book *The Long Bridge*. For a number of years the Woman's Missionary Union prepared and led mission study materials for the local churches. This was done in cooperation with the Home Mission Board and its Annie Armstrong Easter Offering and the Foreign Mission Board and its Lottie Moon Christmas Offering.

The Long Bridge told the story of Dr. Guy Bellamy of Oklahoma and his leadership in ministries of racial reconciliation. He had effectively brought together white, black, Native American, and Hispanic churches in simultaneous revivals as early as 1944. These revivals became building blocks for other ministries of racial reconciliation. Bellamy was the city missions director for the Oklahoma County Association in Oklahoma City, Oklahoma. So effective was Bellamy's work that Dr. J. B. Lawrence, Corresponding Secretary of the Home Mission Board, asked him to join the staff in 1949. Dr. Bellamy did so and was allowed to remain in Oklahoma. From there he traveled the nation by train and car (He despised flying.) as a "goodwill ambassador" and director of the Home Mission Board's Department of Work with Negroes.

The late 1940s was a time of apprehension. Black soldiers were returning from the various theatres of World War II. They were annoyed at having been warmly received in foreign lands, having fought for their country, but being denied basic rights at home. Having been trained in warfare, these men were about to erupt. Bellamy became the prodding voice to Southern Baptists, and a calming voice to blacks through his influence in churches. Among his gifts was the ability to use humor to help his audiences see themselves, and then lay the claims of the gospel upon them.

The Long Bridge, in addition to telling the story of Bellamy's ministry, also made suggestions of how Southern Baptists could take the lead in racial reconciliation. The writer, Phyllis Sapp, picked up the actions some Southern Baptists were beginning to take in addressing their problems with race, mentioning the work of Dr. Nobel Y. Beall of the Home Mission Board; Dr. Frank Leavell, Secretary of Baptist Student Work for the SBC; Drs. T. B. Maston and J. B. Weatherspoon, seminary professors who were ethicists and prodded Southern Baptists. They also worked with Dr. A. C. Miller in helping the Christian Life Commission's emphasis on race to be more accepted. The black persons mentioned in the book were properly addressed by their titles and shown the same respect as others. The book also told of the early organized attempts at racial cooperation: the South-wide Conference Work with Negroes; the Advisory Council of Southern Baptists for Work with Negroes; the American Baptist Theological Seminary Commission; the Department of Work with Negroes, Home Mission Board.

It was the responsibility of the Woman's Missionary Union to write the materials, help the Home Mission Board with the distribution, and lead the teaching of the mission study in local churches. When the book distribution began, the SBC Executive Committee raised loud objections. They did not want "integration" pushed through the SBC. Many members were embroiled in the aftermath of the 1954 Supreme Court decision. Some tried to use old, biblically corrupt interpretations to fight it. The Executive Committee (elected representatives from each state) used its powers to stop further distribution. But copies were already out. (I was a student intern in Louisville, and I still have the copy I was given.) People were teaching it. The furor only made others, who were curious about the book's content, reproduce it in other ways. Some churches were intent on defying the Executive Committee and taught the "mission study" anyhow. These churches were supportive of the Woman's Missionary Union and hated seeing them pushed around. While the Executive Committee had the power in the SBC, the Woman's Missionary Union often had power in the local churches. There was also the growing concern that if the potential for racial conflict was developing, any help in diverting it was welcomed.

As a result of the conflict, the resolve of the Woman's Missionary Union, Home Mission Board, and CLC was strengthened in the fight against racism. These three organizations became allies in future struggles.

Chapter 6

"How Will They Hear without the Preacher?"

The importance of the preacher/pastor in the racial progress Southern Baptists have made cannot be emphasized enough. Throughout the book, references have been made to educators and denominational staffs. Most of these were preachers first. We need to give singular attention to those who remained pastors and church staffers. They were probably in the most vulnerable positions by virtue of being available to individual church members. They also had the greater burden of nourishing or developing their congregations, which required patient skill. There were successes and failures. Some results were not known until long after the efforts had been made.

Many church staff persons and their families carry spiritual and emotional scars from their efforts in racial reconciliation. Some marriages broke up due to the stress caused by "taking a stand." Wives and children felt special isolation when anger was directed toward the pastor. Churches were ill equipped to know how to be supportive to hurting pastors and their families. Some did not want to be supportive. Preferring to be executioners. In the fight between culture and spiritual values, culture often won out.

Many men preached sermons on racism, school integration, open accommodations, and voting rights only to be fired shortly thereafter. I recall a seminary classmate who was tremendously persuaded by Dr. King's sermon at Southern Seminary, April 19, 1961. He shared his "conversion" about race with his congregation the next Sunday. After the sermon, the chair of deacons arose and called the church into conference. Another man presented the motion for dismissal. It was seconded. The church unanimously passed it. The pastor was given his last check and dismissed. With enought research a book could be written on similar incidents.

Unfortunately, the pulpit also represented the other side. Some pastors sided with their church communities and openly supported racist views and acts. One could also begin with the defenses of slavery led by Rev. Richard Furman of South Carolina and continue to more recent years. However, the focus of this book is to tell how Southern Baptists overcame racist domination and altered the essence of their identity.

Any person who was a southern adult in the 1950s, 1960s, and 1970s knows of at least one pastor or church staff person who was abused for taking a positive stand on racial issues. Many people could be included in a book like this. The writer will limit his illustrations to people he knew. These will represent the cadre of those who changed the SBC by their impact on racial issues.

When the writer was pastor in Louisville, Kentucky, William (Bill) Rogers, a classmate at Southern Seminary, was among the first of his friends. Rogers had been preaching and preparing his congregation for school integration. The writer was invited to talk to his congregation. Later, our two churches began holding joint worship services and fellowship opportunities. Other churches, both black and white, started doing the same thing.

Rogers also endeared himself to the writer in a more personal way. The writer was the only African-American student at the seminary in 1960. There were Caribbean and African students on campus, but they were treated differently. Rogers went the second mile in friendship with the writer. Other students took their cue from him and also became friendly.

That friendship was to extend itself in organizational ways. Both of us were on the Joint Committee for the Baptist Fellowship Center, a community center sponsored by the Long Run and Central District Baptist Associations. We were also in the Louisville Baptist Ministers Interracial Fellowship. Our friendship helped smooth the troubled waters of organizational work. Still later, I went to the Home Mission Board, Bill to the Kentucky Baptist Convention staff. We partnered as he directed interracial ministries for the state. William Rogers made a significant contribution to racial reconciliation.

The same can be said for two nearby pastors, Joe Priest Williams and Carlisle Driggers. The proximity of our churches caused us to meet and work on mutual community problems. Our churches were in a racially changing community. Whites were moving out as blacks moved in. Our churches worshiped together, held community meetings, and tackled community issues in an attempt to help bring stability. These churches were open to receive anyone who came. Black people did join their churches. That may have been helped by the fact that we were seen visiting homes together in our neighborhoods. We, too, worked in the Interracial Ministers Conference.

My friendship with Carlisle Driggers took a further dimension. When I became department director at the Home

Mission Board and needed help in addressing both racism and the racially changing communities, I thought immediately of Driggers. He accepted the invitation and worked effectively for three years. Our families traveled together to meetings during the summers and whenever possible. As staff, we traveled together. The public saw blacks and whites in a collegial relationship. Often, we were engaged in conversation by the curious. When Driggers was promoted to a higher administrative position, his attitude did not change. He was in a better position to help promote the work of our division and did so without question. He also continued to challenge racism in the higher echelons of SBC life. Our friendship continues to this day.

Another pastor who significantly challenged Southern Baptists on race was Dr. John Claypool, who pastored one of the very prominent churches in Louisville, Kentucky, Crescent Hill Baptist Church. It was also known as the "seminary" church. It was in close proximity to the seminary, and many students and faculty belonged. Claypool was also an adjunct faculty at Southern. I met him in the coffee shop one morning. He purposely wanted to know me better. That conversation led to a long and meaningful friendship.

Claypool had the idea that with the many Baptist churches and pastors of both races, there were enough people in Louisville to make a difference. We could avoid the turmoil that engulfed many cities in the 1960s. He suggested that we get a small group of pastors together to lay the groundwork for a larger initiative. He suggested six white pastors that he thought would be interested. I suggested six black pastors. We quietly called each man, told them of our idea, and asked for their cooperation. The meetings were held at his home each Tuesday evening for close to six months. The meetings were very honest, open, and frank. No subject was off limits. Included were very aggressive pastors and some who were reticent. We all agreed (1) that school integration was an emotional subject, (2) that we should do all we could to avoid the disruptions that other cities were facing, (3) that we had enough churches and people of goodwill to make a difference, and (4) that we could tackle our other problems resolutely.

At the end of the six months, we felt we had sufficient rapport among the twelve of us that we should approach the respective weekly pastors' conferences of each race, tell them of our plans, and ask them to give up one meeting per month for a new organization to be named the Louisville Baptist Pastors' Interracial Conference. Both conferences agreed. At the organizational meeting, John Claypool was elected chair and I the co-chair.

This conference accomplished a number of projects. We had several public worship services at the Louisville Armory (convention center). Others were held in Walnut Street Baptist Church. We had interracial worship exchanges among churches, project activities among Woman's Missionary Union groups and deacons, choir exchanges, Christmas dinners and parties, many youth activities, public rallies for Open Housing legislation, meetings about zoning problems and "Grandfather Clauses" that were secretly put in place following the severe flood of the late 1930s. Together we challenged the availability of alcoholic outlets in the west end of Louisville. We sponsored job fairs. The greatest thing we did was to establish an openness that had not existed before. Louisville became known as a model city in avoiding the racial clashes that had affected others.

Claypool served as chair of the organization for four years. I followed him and served for two years. We revised the bylaws

limiting officers to two years. In November 1966, Walker
Knight from the Home Mission Board interviewed a group of
us on the successes of the Louisville Baptist Interracial Pastors'
Conference. A spread of several pages appeared in the January
1967 issue of *Home Missions*. That was the same issue that
featured the full-length picture of Dr. William Holmes
Borders on the front cover. The magazine received numerous
cancellations.

John Claypool paid a severe price for his stand on racial
reconciliation. He faced opposition in his church and from the
SBC. All manner of unkind things were said about him, and to
him. His own convention of Baptists turned against him. This
later caused him to become an Episcopalian. It took a long
time, but the postures that Claypool was advocating, for which
he was despised, are now the official positions of the SBC.

I had the privilege of being with Claypool in each of the
other Baptist churches he later served. On those visits, we
relived some of our experiences. More recently, as faculty at
McAfee School of Theology, we found time to reflect on the
years. Amazingly, he was not bitter. He was above that. He saw
a larger purpose in God's gift of grace. We both rejoiced at his
discovery. A great soldier was lost to us with his death in 2005.

There are many other Southern Baptist pastors whom I
have met and who were partners in racial reconciliation. Some
became public representatives. Others were never celebrated.
They found other areas of service, both in and out of the pulpit
ministry. I think of Dr. Thomas J. Holmes, pastor of Tattnall
Square Baptist Church, Macon, Georgia. His story is told in
his book *Ashes for Breakfast*.[36] I met him at a retreat for men

---

[36] Thomas J. Holmes, *Ashes for Breakfast* (Valley Forge PA: Judson Press,
1969).

who had been battered over racial reconciliation. He and his wife shared their agony in the group. We also had other times when we talked privately. His hurt was never relieved.

I think of Dr. D. Perry Ginn when he was pastor of First Baptist Church, Hodgenville, Kentucky. He preached powerful, biblical sermons in the 1950s that dealt with racial injustices and prejudices. He tackled the matter of school desegregation. The whole school system accepted him. He was the baccalaureate speaker for the first integrated school occasion in 1957; he was twenty-seven years old.

Ginn successfully pastored churches in other southern cities that kept "open door" policies for worshipers and membership. He was convincing in his stands against racism and for reconciliation. The secret to his effectiveness was the biblical position he took. He realized that since southern people said they believed the Bible, his job was to make the Bible as plain and authoritative as possible. Any opposition was directed to the Bible, not at him. He is a wise son of the South.

No one should doubt the power of the "spoken word" to affect the end results that God intends. His word does not return void, but accomplishes that which he pleases.

While the focus of this section has been on the contributions of white pastors in the SBC, due diligence must be given to the many African-American pastors who were involved in various ministries of racial reconciliation. Some were strong pulpiteers like Fredrick G. Sampson, Manuel Scott, A. Louis Patterson, Edward V. Hill, Dearing King, Thomas Kilgore, Otis Moss Jr., Sandy Ray, William Jones, and Gardner C. Taylor. Others were men in the trenches: Thurmond Coleman, Lincoln Bingham, Moses Javis, J. Alfred Smith, Edward Davies, George McCalep, Mack King Carter, Charles Boddie, W. J. Hodge, Lewis Lampley, and Alvin

Daniels; and writers such as Henry H. Mitchell, James M. Washington, Gayraud Wilmore, Edward Wheeler, Wyatt Walker, J. DeOtis Roberts, and George Kelsey. This list is not exhaustive. It is not intended to be. It does reflect some of the men who were involved in ministries of racial reconciliation in the SBC during the years of my ministry. Against odds from within the black community, some of them participated in our various conferences and initiatives. They dared to identify with Southern Baptists at a time when ostracism from the black community was frequent. They caught on to Dr. King's idea of the "beloved community" and were willing to help Christ's kingdom to come on earth.

A Vignette

"Sorry, I Forgot to Tell You," Home Missions Week, Ridgecrest, North Carolina, 1983

For twenty-five years I had the joy of teaching in the J terms (January, June, July) at The Southern Baptist Theological Seminary, Louisville, Kentucky. A J term consisted of a student taking one class for a month; often, other guests, such as pastors, denominational leaders, or faculty from other institutions, were invited to teach.

In June 1983, I became friends with a pastor who came to teach "Preaching on Ethical Themes." He was also to be the evening preacher during the July Home Missions Week at Ridgecrest. Having heard that the home missions crowd was an alert group, he asked my help in knowing how to best prepare for the assignment. I told him everything I could think of.

There was, however, one thing that I forgot. I failed to tell him how to respond to the affirmations from black people while he was preaching. The Spillman Auditorium at

Ridgecrest has a U-shaped balcony that begins on one side of the pulpit and wraps around the building to the other side. One of our brothers had taken a front-row seat in the balcony near the pulpit. The preacher was at his best. The brother, attempting to affirm him, said loudly, "That's right. Make it plain, make it plain." The confused preacher looked up at him plaintively and said, "That's what I'm trying to do. Just give me a chance."

A Vignette

"Alright, You Honeymooners," Fall, 1969

Seventeen of the states that took seriously the SBC program of racial reconciliation had a state director. They had various titles—State Director of Work with National Baptists, State Director of Missions, State Director of Interracial Ministries (or Cooperation). In North Carolina, Corbin Cooper was the State Director of Interracial Cooperation.

Corbin planned a series of statewide conferences on racial reconciliation in cooperation with O. L. Sherrill, Executive Director of the General Baptist Convention (National Baptists). The two of them, along with W. R. Grigg, a Home Mission Board staff associate, and myself, spent a week leading nine conferences across the state. We began in the north at Ahoskie with an evening meeting. When it was over, we drove to Wilson for the conference that was to be held that next morning.

We arrived at Wilson well after midnight. Our rooms had been given away. The only two left were one with two double beds and a honeymoon suite. Corbin was in charge of the reservations. He and I had the room with the double beds. The honeymoon suite was given to Grigg and Sherrill.

For blacks and whites to share the same room was unheard of in 1969.

Our rooms were on the inside courtyard next to the pool. On the other side of the pool was the restaurant. Corbin and I came out of our room first the next morning as we prepared to go to breakfast. Those around the pool and those looking from the restaurant acted as though aliens from another planet had arrived when they saw a black man and a white man coming out of the same room. The honeymoon suite was on the second floor above us. Since Grigg and Sherrill were late, Corbin called out to them, "Alright, you honeymooners, come on down." About three minutes later, Grigg and Sherrill, both men who weighed around 250 pounds, emerged from the suite. The shock wave would have exceeded number ten on the Richter Scale!

A Vignette

"The Power of a Layman"

Mr. Owen Cooper, Yazoo City, Mississippi, was a powerful layman in Mississippi and in the SBC. He led the fight against adopting "the Statement on the Crisis in the Nation" in the Houston convention, June 1968. He later had a conversion in his attitude. He then became a staunch promoter for racial reconciliation.

In December 1968, Cooper met with W. R. Grigg, my colleague at the Home Mission Board, W. P. Davis and Richard Brogan of the Mississippi Baptist State Convention, and me. Out of that meeting came the conviction that since preachers were dismissed or otherwise brutally treated for preaching about racism, that laypeople should take up the cause. No one would fire them.

Cooper suggested that we have a Bible study retreat for laymen in Mississippi. We agreed. The retreat was scheduled for January 17–18, 1969, at the black-owned Sophia Sutton Assembly in Prentiss, Mississippi. Cooper was to invite the Southern Baptists, and Davis the National Baptists.

On the date of the retreat, approximately 240 black and white men showed up at the assembly. The meeting started before room assignments were given. Cooper and Davis had intentionally mixed up the assignments. This was explained to the men following a Bible study on reconciliation. A few men were angry or scared and left, but most stayed. By the end of the first evening, we were relaxed and began to enter into the spirit of the event.

Owen Cooper got our attention by pointing to two areas that affected most in the room—progressive farming and better housing. Cooper owned a fertilizer company and supplied most of the state and region. By the time the meeting ended, he had led the formation of both a farm cooperative and a housing cooperative. He found common needs and created reconciliation in response to those needs.

Cooper later used his own resources to travel the nation to share his experience with others through the SBC Brotherhood. He involved himself in the reconciliation work of the Home Mission Board and expansive work of the Baptist World Alliance. During his two years as president of the SBC, it was my joy to travel with him to meetings of the three National Baptist conventions. As he told his "Damascus Road" conversion at the point of race, black leadership enthusiastically embraced him.

Cooper had talked of retiring from his business and devoting himself to ministries of racial reconciliation. Death interrupted his plans.

Chapter 7

The Lord Works in Mysterious Ways: Meeting Governor George Wallace

In April 1978 Carlisle Driggers planned a conference in Birmingham, Alabama. The conference, "The Church in the Racially Changing Community," was planned for the Hyatt Hotel Convention Center.

Two weeks prior to the meeting, Jack Brymer, editor of the *Alabama Baptist* and president of the Baptist Press Association, called with a concern. His association was meeting in the same hotel at the same time as our conference. About 125 people would be in their conference. Ours was expecting close to 500 from across the nation. The concern was not the logistics of space. They had invited Governor George Wallace to speak in their meeting. They wanted to find out the mind of a "populace." How did Governor Wallace command the attention and loyalty he had? We, of course, were interested in the same thing. Rather than conjecture, our staff wanted to hear from the man himself.

We assured Brymer that instead of being offended, we wished to join them in the conference. Since we had the larger space, we agreed that they would join us.

When we announced to our conference at the opening session that Governor Wallace would be speaking at a joint meeting, some of our group were offended. They spared no words in criticizing our desire to learn how the mind of a man like Wallace worked. Our staff remained steadfast in our decision.

There was an understanding with the press association that Governor Wallace would deliver his speech and we would have a question-and-answer session. I would have the closing words with the opportunity to respond with a positive word when the session was concluding.

When Governor Wallace was wheeled in, the sight of the man evoked sympathy. Crippled by an assassin's bullet in Maryland, he was totally dependent on others. It was obvious he was under medication to ease his pain. His hearing was almost gone. An associate stood near him to write down what he could not hear. Occasionally he yelled in the governor's ear.

Wallace won the sympathy of the group by apologizing for the harm he had done. He named and categorized the things he had done. He interpreted the sniper's bullet as being like the bright light that knocked the Apostle Paul down on the road to Damascus. Now, even though maimed, he wanted God to use what was left of him.

As I looked around the room, handkerchiefs were wiping tears from many eyes. Even some who had criticized us were crying. Later they apologized publicly for their attitudes. Governor Wallace taught us what redemptive grace was all about. He also reminded us of that divine justice is alive. He was a public illustration of it.

Our group never would have had that experience had it not been for the "mysterious way" in which God works.

Chapter 8

The *Becoming* Incident
December 2, 1971

"Big Georgian Making Big Changes in Nashville" was the headline in the Georgia Baptist *Christian Index*, announcing the departure of one of its pastors from the Waldrop Memorial Baptist Church, Columbus, to a position on the Sunday School Board, Nashville, Tennessee. This position, Director of the Church Materials and Services Division, placed Dr. Alan B. Comish in authority next to the Executive Director, Dr. James L. Sullivan.

Since 1968, the Sunday School Board had complied with the SBC request related to implementing *The Statement on the Crisis in the Nation*. It reproduced and distributed the document and developed materials for the Sunday school and church training programs that dealt with racial reconciliation. Its college student department not only produced materials, but in its summer conferences trained those who would be leading state student emphases in dealing with progressive racial programs.

"The *Becoming* Incident" refers to a quarterly named *Becoming*, designed for fourteen- and fifteen-year-old youths. Twyla Wright of Casa Grande, Arizona, wrote this material. I was fortunate to have been on one of the teams writing for church training. I remember how in our writer's retreat we agonized over each other's assignments, offering suggestions that would enable us to produce quality work.

After the material had been printed, 140,000 copies of *Becoming* were recalled. The official statement was that the content on race was subject to misinterpretation. A couple paragraphs from Wright's work were replaced by a comparable paragraph that had previously been written from another quarterly. Bob Terry, then editor of the *Word and Way*, the Missouri state Baptist paper, did a parallel comparison of what Wright had written and the substituted paragraphs. His comparison appeared in the Georgia *Christian Index*, January 1, 1972. From his comparison, the material Wright had written was less caustic than that which was substituted.

As others weighed in on the controversy, the general consensus was that the real objection was the picture on the front cover. The picture had been purchased from a freelance photographer named Rhon Engh of Star Prairie, Wisconsin. Taken at Hamblin College, St. Paul, Minnesota, the photograph showed a black male student talking to two white female students in front of a column of a campus building. They were standing more than five feet from each other and appeared to be in serious conversation.

The explanations for withdrawing the issue offered by the Sunday School Board leadership did not satisfy the Southern Baptist public. The state Baptist papers from Kentucky, District of Columbia, Virginia, California, North Carolina, Georgia, Maryland, Northwest Convention, Texas, and Illinois wrote articles condemning the Sunday School Board's action. Only four states supported them: Alabama, Mississippi, South Carolina, and Tennessee.

The Baptist State Student Conventions of Texas, North Carolina, and South Carolina, publicly opposed the action. Over 400 letters were sent to the Sunday School Board. Only eighty-six supported them. Twenty state Baptist conventions passed resolutions opposing the action.

Unfortunately, Frank Grayum, editor of *Becoming*, resigned. There remained speculation on whether his resignation was forced or of his own volition. Grayum, a graduate of William Jewell College and Midwestern Seminary, was an excellent literary craftsman.

Baptist Press, the official news agency of the SBC, was disturbed because the *Religious News Service* and the *Washington Post* broke the news items to the public instead of them. "Why?"

The image of a great statesman and leader, Dr. James Sullivan, was sullied by this incident. He had been a friend to his colleagues in the two National Baptist (black) publishing houses, also in Nashville. He offered technical support, camaraderie, and the Sunday School Board's resources to assist their efforts. Long before other public restaurants were open to blacks in Nashville, the Sunday School Board's cafeteria was open. Sullivan died on December 27, 2004, at age ninety-four. An *Associated Press* article dated January 4, 2005, noted that his family said he was often maligned for his position on race as a result of this incident. Dr. Jimmy Draper, president of the Sunday School Board, in the same news release said, "He led in the production of materials promoting the Biblical view of human worth regardless of race, and modeled his beliefs by providing an equitable work environment for a multi-cultural staff."[37]

The negative publicity from the secular press was a great embarrassment to Southern Baptists. Despite visits to colleges and seminaries to explain, apologize, and test the pulse of the public, Southern Baptists were offended.

It is this writer's opinion that one of the great turning points for Southern Baptists in moving toward a healthier attitude about race was the *Becoming* incident. Southern Baptists were headed in the direction of improved racial attitudes for which there was no turning back.

A Vignette

"As We Checked Out, They Checked In," July 4th Week, 1975

As the new director of the Department of Cooperative Ministries with National Baptists, I desired to get to know the state directors and their families better. They were invited to spend the week of July 4 at Stone Mountain, Georgia. The twenty-two men and their families, plus our staff, gave us a crowd of about 135 people.

Edward Wheeler, associate director in our office, planned the evening devotionals. He scouted around and found an outside area that would allow privacy and the opportunity to enjoy nature. Everything went well as far as the spiritual experiences were concerned. But the next morning, after the outdoor setting, everyone was

---

[37] Greg Warner, "Baptist Statesman, James Sullivan, 94, former Sunday School Board head, dies," *Associated Baptist Press*, January 4, 2005. <www.ABPNews.com>

complaining of the insect bites. The rock slabs on which we sat had an abundance of chiggers. Finally, one teenage daughter stood up and said, "This is a shame. Here we are, black and white, trying to learn how to defeat racism, and you all can't even talk right. It's not 'Chiggers'; it's 'Chigroes.'"

Another irony of that week was that our meeting finished on the morning of Friday, July 3. As we were checking out of the Stone Mountain Inn, the Ku Klux Klan was checking in for one of their weekend rallies on the backside of Stone Mountain.

Chapter 9

A Statement Concerning
the Crisis in Our Nation
June 5, 1958

Passing resolutions is a part of the agenda of annual SBC meetings. Resolutions express the sentiments of the majority of those gathered at that particular convention. They may or may not represent the sentiments of the people in the churches from which the messengers came. These resolutions are not binding; that is to say, they cannot be enforced. The extent to which they are publicized depends on the denominational political climate, the attitudes of the state convention leadership, as well as local associations and churches.

In 1947, Southern Baptists passed a resolution, "The Charter of Principles on Race Relations," at the annual meeting in St. Louis, Missouri. This resolution came on the heels of President Harry Truman's (a Baptist) proclamation that desegregated the Armed Forces. It also represented a desire to suppress the growing discomfort of black soldiers returning from World War II.

More importantly, the resolution was prompted by the Baptist Joint Committee on Public Relations, a consortia of Baptist conventions in the United States, including the two major black conventions. This organization was created in

1946. Southern Baptists were represented by its agency, the Social Service Commission (later named the Christian Life Commission). The Social Service Commission presented the following resolution to the SBC:

The Charter of Principles on Race Relations
(1) We shall think of the Negro as a person and treat him accordingly.
(2) We shall continually strive as individuals to conquer prejudice and eliminate from our speech terms of contempt and from our conduct actions of ill will.
(3) We shall teach our children that prejudice is un-Christian.
(4) We shall protest against injustice and indignities against Negroes, as we do in the case of people of our own race, wherever and whenever we meet them.
(5) We shall be willing for the Negro to enjoy the rights granted to him under the Constitution of the United States, including the right to vote, to serve on juries, to receive justice in the courts, to be free from mob violence, to secure a just share of the benefits of educational and other funds, and to receive equal service for equal treatment on public carriers and conveniences.
(6) We shall be just in our dealing with the Negro as an individual. Whenever he is in our employ we shall pay him an adequate wage and provide for him healthful working conditions.
(7) We shall strive to promote community goodwill between the races in every way possible.
(8) We shall actively cooperate with Negro Baptists in the building up of their churches, the education of their

ministers, and the promotion of their missions and evangelistic programs.[38]

This resolution did not have the impact that the resolution of 1968 was to have. It may have been the strongest declaration for racial justice made by Southern Baptists up to that time. The 1968 statement came after several years of racial turmoil, including the attempts to desegregate public schools, achieve public accommodations, voting rights, and other attempts at overcoming racial barriers.

More tragically, the resolution of 1968 followed the assassinations of Dr. Martin Luther King Jr. and Senator Robert F. Kennedy. A large contingent of white students, called Baptist Students Concerned, staged a silent vigil throughout the SBC meetings at Houston, Texas. Their placards called attention to the problems of race, poverty, and war.[39]

The resolution, "A Statement Concerning the Crisis in Our Nation," marked the combined efforts of more than thirty state executive directors, editors of state Baptist papers, denominational agency leaders, pastors, and seminary professors. The document is reprinted in its entirety.

Statement Concerning the Crisis in Our Nation
June 5, 1968

---

[38] George Kelsey, *Social Ethics Among Southern Baptists, 1917–1968* (Metuchen NJ: Scarecrow Press, 1973) 251–52.

[39] John Lee Eighmy, *Churches in Cultural Captivity: A History of the Social Attitudes of Southern Baptists* (Knoxville: University of Tennessee Press, 1972) 198.

We Face a Crisis. Our nation is enveloped in a social and cultural revolution. We are shocked by the potential for anarchy in a land dedicated to democracy and freedom. There are ominous sounds of hate and violence among men and of unbelief and rebellion toward God. These compel Christians to face the social situation and to examine themselves under the judgment of God.

We are an affluent society, abounding in wealth and luxury. Yet far too many of our people suffer from poverty. Many are hurt by circumstances from which they find it most difficult to escape, injustice which they find most difficult to correct, or heartless exploitation which they find most difficult to resist. Many live in slum housing or ghettos of race or poverty or ignorance or bitterness that often generate both despair and defiance.

We are a nation that declares the sovereignty of law and the necessity of civil order. Yet we have had riots and have tolerated conditions that breed riots, spread violence, foster disrespect for the law, and undermine the democratic process.

We are a nation that declares the equality and rights of persons irrespective of race. Yet, as a nation, we have allowed cultural patterns to persist that have deprived millions of black Americans, and other racial groups as well, of equality of recognition and opportunity in the areas of education, employment, citizenship, housing, and worship. Worse still, as a nation, we have condoned prejudices that have damaged the personhood of blacks and whites alike. We have seen a climate of racism and reactionism develop resulting in hostility, injustice, suspicion, faction, strife, and alarming potential for bitterness, division, destruction, and death.

We Review Our Efforts. In the face of national shortcomings, we must nevertheless express appreciation for men of goodwill of all races and classes who have worked tirelessly and faithfully to create a Christian climate in our nation.

From the beginning of the Southern Baptist Convention, and indeed in organized Baptist life, we have affirmed God's love for all men of all continents and colors, of all regions and races. We have continued to proclaim that the death of Jesus on Calvary's cross is the instrument of God's miraculous redemption for every individual.

Inadequately but sincerely, we have sought in our nation and around the world both to proclaim the gospel to the lost and to minister to human needs in Christ's name. Individually and collectively, we are trying to serve, but we have yet to use our full resources to proclaim the gospel whereby all things are made new in Christ.

We Voice Our Confession. "If my people, which are called by my name, shall humble themselves, and pray, and seek my face, and turn from their wicked ways; then will I hear from heaven, and will forgive their sin, and will heal their land" (2 Chron. 7:14).

The current crisis arouses the Christian conscience. Judgment begins at the house of God. Christians are inescapably involved in the life of the nation. Along with all other citizens we recognize our share of responsibility for creating in our land conditions in which justice, order, and righteousness can prevail. May God forgive us wherein we have failed him and our fellowman.

As Southern Baptists, representative of one of the largest bodies of Christians in our nation and claiming special ties of spiritual unity with the large conventions of Negro Baptists in our land, we have come far short of our privilege in Christian brotherhood.

Humbling ourselves before God, we implore him to create in us a right spirit of repentance and to make us instruments of his redemption, his righteousness, his peace, and his love toward all men.

We Declare Our Commitment. The Christ we serve, the opportunity we face, and the crises we confront compel us to action. We therefore declare our commitment, believing this to be right in the sight of God and our duty under the lordship of Christ.

We will respect every individual as a person possessing inherent dignity and worth growing out of his creation in the image of God.

We will strive to obtain and secure for every person the equality of human and legal rights. We will undertake to secure opportunities in matters of citizenship, public services, education, employment, and personal habitation that every man may achieve his highest potential as a person.

We will accept and exercise our civic responsibility as Christians to defend people against injustice. We will strive to insure for all persons the full opportunity for achievement according to the endowments given by God.

We will refuse to be a party to any movement that fosters racism or violence or mob action.

We will personally accept every Christian as a brother beloved in the Lord and welcome to the fellowship of faith and worship every person irrespective of race or class.

We will strive by personal initiative and every appropriate means of communication to bridge divisive barriers, to work for reconciliation, and to open channels of fellowship and cooperation.

We will strive to become well informed about public issues, social ills, and divisive movements that are damaging to human relationships. We will strive to resist prejudice and to combat forces that breed distrust and hostility.

We will recognize our involvement with other Christians and with all others of goodwill in the obligation to work for righteousness in public life and justice for all persons. We will strive to promote Christian brotherhood as a witness to the gospel of Christ.

We Make an Appeal. Our nation is at the crossroads. We must decide whether we shall be united in goodwill, freedom, and justice under God to serve mankind or be destroyed by covetousness, passion, hate, and strife.

We urge all leaders and supporters of minority groups to encourage their followers to exercise Christian concern and respect for the person and property of others and to manifest the responsible action commensurate with individual dignity and Christian citizenship.

We appeal to our fellow Southern Baptists to join us in self-examination under the Spirit of God and to accept the present crisis as a challenge from God to strive to reconciliation by love.

We appeal to our fellow Southern Baptists to engage in Christian ventures in human relationships, and to take courageous actions for justice and peace.

We believe that a vigorous Christian response to this national crisis is imperative for an effective witness on our part at home and abroad.

Words will not suffice. The time has come for action. Our hope for healing and renewal is in the redemption of the whole of life. Let us call men to faith in Christ. Let us dare to accept the challenge.

We therefore recommend to the messengers of the Southern Baptist Convention that:

1. We approve this statement on the national crisis.

2. We rededicate ourselves to the proclamation of the gospel, which includes redemption of the individual and his involvement in the social issues of our day.

3. We request the Home Mission Board to take the leadership in working with the Convention agencies concerned with the problems related to this crisis in the most effective manner possible and in keeping with their program assignments.

4. We call upon individuals, the churches, the associations, and the state conventions to join the Southern Baptist Convention in a renewal of Christian effort to meet the national crisis.

(We recognize that no individual or organization can speak for all Baptists. The following represents the concern, confession, commitment, and appeal by the majority of the messengers meeting in Houston, Texas, June 5, 1968.)

Following a four-hour contest of wills, the resolution passed. Significantly, one of the men who opposed the statement later became a leader in race relations in the SBC. As a layman, Owen Cooper (Mississippi), noted that laypeople would not be put out of their churches as their pastors were for championing race relations. He issued a call to Southern Baptist laity to take up the cause of racial justice. He was a brave and daring man who knew how to get the attention of those considered racist.

The editors of state Baptist papers also contributed to promoting the resolution. I mention in particular John J. Hurt, Georgia; Reuben Alley, Virginia; Chauncey Daley, Kentucky; Terry Young, California; J. Marse Grant, North Carolina; E. S. James, Texas; and Erwin McDonald, Arkansas. There were probably others of whom I am not aware. Their work through the Baptist Press did much to inform and change Southern Baptist thought and practice.

This writer agrees with John L. Eighmy's opinion that the 1968 resolution did much to change the direction of Southern Baptists regarding race. I was elected by the Home Mission Board in May 1968. When I began, there was an eagerness in SBC churches to get on with the agenda. At least eight churches in Atlanta invited our family to place our membership with them. Invitations to preach or lecture from churches, associations, and conferences were plentiful. In most places I went, there was a readiness for racial reconciliation. The agencies of the SBC requested our help in redirecting their programs to become inclusive. A new day had dawned!

Chapter 10

The Christian Life Commission
An Ethical Conscience

Samuel Hill suggests that southerners lived apart from major developments in the world during the nineteenth and twentieth centuries. The disassociation with other cultures allowed an emphasis on individualism. Southern Baptists had to struggle to think socially. Southern-ness and Christianity have been overlaid. Each supports the other.[40]

Southern Baptists did have social concerns, but they were selective: temperance, separation of church and state, Sabbath conduct, legalized gambling, and obscenity. The organization assigned the responsibility of leading Southern Baptists in ethical and social awareness was the Christian Life Commission. The 1907, the SBC annual noted a call for an organization to deal with civic righteousness. In 1908, the Standing Committee on Temperance was formed to deal with the use and abuse of alcohol.[41]

---

[40] John Lee Eighmy, *Churches in Cultural Captivity: A History of the Social Attitudes of Southern Baptists* (Knoxville: University of Tennessee Press; rev. Samuel Hill, 1987) 201–203.

[41] H. Leon McBeth, *The Baptist Heritage* (Nashville TN: Broadman Press, 1987) 656.

The organization that became the forerunner of the later Christian Life Commission was the Social Service Commission, in 1913. The chair was W. L. Poteat, and the commission combined the emphases on temperance with the concern against lynching. Arthur J. Barton, who was the first field staff of the Home Mission Board to work with blacks, led the charge supporting this emphasis.[42]

From its earliest days, the commission was not popular in the SBC. Dr. Leon McBeth includes a suggestion that the dispensational and pre-millennial doctrines of the SBC may have discouraged extensive attention to social concerns: "Those who expect the speedy end of the world are less concerned to improve it."[43] That may be so, but I am of a different opinion. Because the early emphases of the Christian Life Commission and its antecedents also emphasized racial justice and fairness, and because of the early teachings about racial superiority/inferiority, and because of the attempts to justify slavery, the attitudes toward the Christian Life Commission may have been carryovers from those against abolitionists or anyone else trying to change life in the South. The SBC's official policy mirrored popular opinion.

In 1933, Edwin McNeill Poteat Jr. proposed the SBC create "an agency of Social Research" to study social problems and plan concerted action. His proposal was rejected by the SBC.[44]

Following the death of A. J. Barton in 1942, J. B. Weatherspoon became chairman of the Social Service Commission and served until 1955, a very dynamic time for the

---

[42] Ibid.
[43] Ibid.
[44] Ibid.

commission. For instance, in 1946 there was a call for a broader social awareness in the SBC and a plan of action.[45] In 1947, the Social Service Commission was strengthening by employing a full-time director. (Hugh A. Brimm became that person and served until 1953.)[46] That same year, the Christian Life Commission presented to the SBC a Charter of Principles on Race Relations. It also praised the desegregation in colleges, professional organizations, and labor unions. It opposed discrimination in voting, education, and employment.[47]

In 1953, Acker C. Miller joined the staff (and served until 1960),[48] and the Social Service Commission changed its name to the Christian Life Commission.[49] The following year, the Christian Life Commission supported *Brown v. Board*. They did this by encouraging the SBC to support civil authority, calling it a moral obligation by the largest religious body in the South.[50] The Weatherspoon years also saw the influence of men like T. B. Maston, Olin Blinkley, Das Kelly Barnett, Joseph M. Dawson, and C. Emmanuel Carlson.

During his presidency of the SBC (1958–1959), Senator Brooks Hays of Arkansas presented progressive racial views. As a member of the Christian Life Commission Board, he used this position to push his racial views forward. Those views cost him the end of his political career.[51]

---

[45] Ibid., 656–57.

[46] Ibid., 657.

[47] Eighmy, *Churches in Cultural Captivity*, 189.

[48] McBeth, *The Baptist Heritage*, 657.

[49] Ibid.

[50] Eighmy, *Churches in Cultural Captivity*, 189.

[51] Terry Goddard, "Southern Social Justice: Brooks Hays and the Little Rock School Crisis," *Baptist History & Heritage* (Spring 2003): 68–85.

In 1960, Dr. Foy Valentine became director of Christian Life Commission.[52] He was a protégé of Dr. T. B. Maston at Southwestern Baptist Theological Seminary. Valentine built a quality staff that led conferences, wrote materials and books, preached, lectured, and lobbied for ethical issues, especially race. The summer assemblies at state conventions, and the national centers at Ridgecrest, North Carolina, and Glorieta, New Mexico, became places where the tradition was challenged. The budget SBC allotted to the Christian Life Commission did not provide for field staff. A partnership between the Home Mission Board and the Christian Life Commission allowed the mission staff of the Home Mission Board to use the materials and resources the Christian Life Commission provided. This enabled the Christian Life Commission's messages to move across the SBC.

Foy Valentine was the Christian Life Commission's "David," fighting the SBC's "Goliath" of racism. His personal manifesto was, "I shall neither withdraw from the world nor be conformed to it. This means I must daily bear the cross; and this I do, if not always gladly, then at least always resolutely."[53] This he did in the midst of name-calling, plots to have him fired, personal insults, and opposition to the Christian Life Commission.

The affirmations and high moments of his ministry were few. One of them was when Valentine led a Christian Citizenship Seminar for denominational leaders in Washington, D.C., 1964. President Lyndon Johnson invited the group to

---

[52] Jesse Fletcher, *The Southern Baptist Convention* (Nashville TN: Broadman Press, 1994) 200.

[53] William T. Moore, *His Heart Is Black* (Atlanta GA: Home Mission Board, 1979) 69.

the White House. He also solicited their help in getting the Civil Rights Bill passed.

Another affirmation came when a prominent member of the SBC Executive Committee attempted to abolish the Christian Life Commission. Valentine successfully convinced the brother in the error of his thinking. That led to the same man opening a way for the Christian Life Commission's program to be presented in his state and support for increasing the Christian Life Commission's budget, including adding additional staff.[54] Yet another affirmation was the SBC's passing of the 1968 "Crisis Statement," which Valentine and Clifton Allen drafted.

The ministry of Dr. Foy Valentine was used of God to help prepare the SBC for the 1995 statement. Although he was not a participant on the committee, he laid the groundwork.

In 1961, the SBC assigned the Christian Life Commission two functions: (1) to assist the churches by helping them understand the moral demands of the gospel and, (2) to help Southern Baptists to apply Christian principles to moral and social problems. The Christian Life Commission made use of a motto: "Helping changed people to change the world."[55]

The Christian Life Commission had the support of faculties who had been trained in Baptist colleges and seminaries, by such men as those previously mentioned. The list of others who joined their ranks is extensive. They included those in ethics, Bible, pastoral care, theology, and missions. Many students had their previous notions about race challenged. Some were freed by their new information. Others were confused and bewildered. The classroom impressions

---

[54] Ibid., 68.
[55] McBeth, *The Baptist Heritage*, 657.

were bolstered by the chapel speakers, special lecturers, conferences, retreats, and public news events. Pastors who were courageous enough to stand against the tide also became role models for students. This mighty army went forth to "help changed people change the world."

"Race Relations Day," an annual event each February, although not popular, did make a contribution to race relations. It offered those who wanted to make a statement an opportunity to do so in a variety of ways, including emphases in worship services, pulpit exchanges, choir worship, service projects, and observing black history. Some renamed it "Groundhog Day," a time when the issue of race relations popped up and was put to rest for another year.

In 1989, Dr. Richard Land became the director of the Christian Life Commission. One of the first things he did was to assemble the black staffs of all SBC national agencies to plan a coordinated effort in promoting racial reconciliation. That meeting resulted in a national conference scheduled around Dr. King's birthday celebration in January 1990.

The 1995 statement was one of the significant accomplishments of the Christian Life Commission. It is treated in a separate section of this book.

Perhaps one of the strongest speeches this writer has heard a Southern Baptist denominational executive deliver on race was given by Dr. Land at the Baptist World Alliance's Summit on Racism and Ethnic Cleansing, January, 8, 1999, at the Ebenezer Baptist Church, Atlanta, Georgia. It was convincingly powerful. The Ethics and Religious Liberty Commission (new name for the Christian Life Commission) continues to give leadership to the SBC in matters of race. However, it is not alone. Every entity of the SBC is involved in racial and ethnic inclusiveness in one way or another. Racism still exists in the SBC. It, like all other sin, will be with us until Jesus returns, but it is no longer an accepted norm.

A Vignette

"Brother's Keepers?" A Hotel Conference Room, Asheville, North Carolina, August 20, 1968

It was my first meeting with the state directors of Work with National Baptists. These were white Southern Baptists from seventeen states. In addition, there were three of us from the Home Mission Board department staff and one executive director from a National Baptist (black) state convention. The meeting was about how to do racial reconciliation and help white and black groups work together in the states that were part of the SBC.

I was the new entity in the equation. Much had been publicized about the "first black" elected to an executive position in the SBC. The men were eyeing me curiously. Across the table sat a short fellow with squinting eyes, a full head of white hair, and a reddish face. His appearance, his continual squinting, and his Mississippi heritage raised negative concerns in me.

As the meeting progressed, one of the men used the worn-out cliché of that day: "We are our brother's keepers." The man from Mississippi bolted straight up in his seat and protested, "We are not our brother's keepers. I wish you all would read your Bibles correctly. That's not what Genesis 4:1–14 says. Here, I've turned to my Bible. Let's read that passage together."

The lesson continued: "Nowhere in there does God tell us that I am or you are our brother's keepers. That was Cain's smart aleck reply when God questioned him about Abel. We are not our brother's keepers. If anything, we ought to be our brother's brother. I have no business trying to 'keep' any other person. If I 'keep' you, I control you. If I 'brother' you, I allow you the freedom to develop as God wants you to. My job is to see that you can be all you can be and help you to become."

After that speech he relaxed in his chair, looked me dead in the eye, winked, and a smile lit up his face. William P. Davis and I became the best of friends, even until his death.

Chapter 11

The Home Mission Board:
Catalyst for Racial Reconciliation

In his book *Mission to America*, Dr. Arthur B. Rutledge says, "In 1800 only about five percent of Negroes in the United States were professing Christians. The population was growing rapidly and the evangelistic challenge was immense. In Augusta, Georgia in 1845, in its organizational meeting, the SBC instructed the newly formed Domestic Mission Board 'to take all prudent measures for the religious instruction of our colored people.'"[56]

In the years between 1845 to the late 1890s, the Domestic Mission Board (later named the Home Mission Board) directed the SBC with the black population. This included advocacy for evangelizing the black population, recognizing the "called" among them, providing opportunities for training, purchasing the freedom of slave preachers, and helping black churches get started.

They had to overcome the lingering notion of "soul inferiority" and the refusal of some whites to recognize the personhood of blacks. The Great Awakening revivals showed

---

[56] Arthur B. Rutledge, *Mission to America: A Century and a Quarter of Southern Baptist Home Missions* (Nashville TN: Broadman Press, 1969) 130.

the "mysterious ways God moved." During those protracted meetings, slaves who were there to tend to the needs of their masters and their families got caught up in the same religious phenomena as the whites. They were shouting, jerking, barking, and expressing religious fervor. Now that their religious capacity for salvation was recognized by whites, the White religious leaders had to reckon with the sameness.

The suggestion in the first paragraph that in 1800 only five percent of the black population was Christian does not recognize another reality. Slaves were also worshiping secretly at night in "hush harbors or brush harbors." There is no data capable of documenting those numbers. More recent research suggests that some brought an awareness of Christianity with them from Africa and may have continued those practices in secret. There were also those whose masters forbade them to worship, so they worshiped secretly.

Exceptions to this cultural ban did occur, however. For instance, in 1849 Rev. Noah Davis, a black man, was pastoring and church planting under the supervision of the Maryland Baptist Union Association (state convention). In 1828 the Montgomery County Baptist Association (Alabama) purchased the freedom of Caesar McLemore so that he could preach. In 1845 the Concord Association of United Baptists in Tennessee purchased the freedom of Edmund Kelley for the preaching of the gospel.[57] Of course, the story of John Jasper in Virginia is legendary. He was baptized in February 1840 and began preaching that afternoon. He became the preferred preacher at funerals in the nearby counties, even preferred above white

---

[57] Ibid., 129–30.

preachers. His lasting fame was at Sixth Mount Zion Baptist Church, Richmond.[58]

The Board of Domestic Missions began appointing missionaries to the black population in 1848. By 1859 it is estimated that there were nearly 400,000 professing black Baptists.[59] The strongest numbers came from South Carolina, Georgia, Alabama, Mississippi, Kentucky, Virginia, North Carolina, Tennessee, and eastern Ohio.[60]

Growth among black Baptists was fast for several reasons: (1) Baptists did not have literacy requirements for membership. A testimony of saving grace was all that was necessary for both church membership and the ministry; (2) freedom from judicatory regulations or other structures appealed to both whites and blacks in the South; (3) worship allowed creativity of and for expression; (4) the mystical rites of baptism and the Lord's Supper appealed to the African heritage; (5) the emotionalism of Baptist worship was akin to the African heritage. In some instances the number of worshiping blacks exceeded the whites. In 1850, the Georgia Association (Georgia Baptist Convention) had forty-five churches with 2,815 white members and 3,908 black members. Ten years later, there were forty-six churches with 3,112 white members and 5,052 black members. Since these churches were in the SBC, it can be honestly said that there have been black Southern Baptists since the beginning of the SBC.[61]

---

[58] Richard Ellsworth Day, *Rhapsody in Black: The Life Story of John Jasper* (Valley Forge PA: Judson Press, 1953).

[59] B. D. Ragsdale, *The Story of Georgia Baptists* (Atlanta GA: Executive Committee of the Georgia Baptist Convention, 1938) 3:65.

[60] Lerone Bennett, *Before the Mayflower: A History of the Negro in America, 1619–1954* (New York: Penguin Books, 1966) 234.

[61] Rutledge, *Mission to America*, 131.

In some instances, slaves were allowed to separate from white churches to form their own congregations. One such illustration is the Fifth Street Baptist Church, Louisville, Kentucky. In 1829, eighteen slaves were permitted to separate from the First Baptist Church (now Walnut Street Baptist Church). A second group left First Baptist and formed the Green Street Baptist Church in 1844.[62]

Even before the formation of Fifth Street Baptist Church, there were other separate black churches. Among them were the "Bluestone" Church on the William Byrd Plantation, Mecklenburg, Virginia (1758), and the Silver Bluff Baptist Church, South Carolina, which started between 1773 and 1775. The First African Baptist Church, Savannah, Georgia (1788), is considered the oldest church in continual existence, started by black people.[63]

Post-Civil War Changes

The Civil War brought changes in religious activities. The agendas for blacks and whites differed. Whites were concerned about rebuilding the destruction that plagued the South. Blacks were focused on the "uplift of the race": finding land to own, gathering equipment, building homes, securing education, learning trade skills, dealing with an increasingly hostile white society, and negotiating options for survival.

These changes led many blacks to voluntarily withdraw from white churches and form their own. In some instances, they were forced to leave. Assisting the development of

---

[62] Emmanuel McCall, *Centennial Volume: General Association of Kentucky Baptists* (Louisville KY: Standard Press, 1968) 148, 170.

[63] C. Eric Lincoln and Lawrence Mamiya, *The Black Church in the African-American Experience* (Durham NC: Duke University Press, 1990) 24–25.

southern blacks were the Home Mission societies of Northern Baptists. They helped build schools, colleges, and seminaries, and they assisted the efforts of black denominations. Because Southern Baptists had their own agenda and because of the animosity some felt toward the North, these activities were allowed, although not appreciated.

Southern Baptists did help in occasional ways, such as joining with Northern Baptists in some educational efforts. In 1884, R. T. Pollard of Alabama became the first black SBC missionary, serving as a theological professor.[64]

In 1895 Southern and Northern Baptists cooperated in developing the New Era Plan. This was a financial and programmatic effort to support struggling black churches and denominational units. With the organization of the National Baptist Convention that year, Southern Baptists modified the New Era Plan as an instrument of their cooperation. Southern Baptists appointed a full-time field director, Arthur Barton, as Secretary for Negro Work. By 1905 the two conventions had thirty-three appointed missionaries. By 1914, that number had increased to forty-seven. This effort continued until 1923 when Southern Baptists began having financial difficulties.[65]

By 1937 Southern Baptists had recovered financially and reorganized the program as the Department of Cooperative Work with Negroes. Noble Y. Beall of Alabama became the director. Teacher missionaries were again appointed.[66]

In 1942, both the Southern Baptist Home Mission Board and the American Baptist Board of Education joined in the support of Beall. Northern Baptists had ten black institutions

---

[64] Rutledge, *Mission to America*, 131.
[65] Ibid., 134.
[66] Ibid., 135.

in the South that needed general supervision. Beall employed the first black staff member of the Home Mission Board, Dr. Roland Smith, in 1942. When Beall resigned in 1945, Smith became special assistant to the executive secretary, where he served until 1949.[67]

In 1949, Dr. Guy Bellamy was elected secretary (director) of Negro Work. This was a turbulent era during which soldiers were returning from World War II, angered by the way they were treated in the United States. Mechanized farming lessened the need for workers in the South. Many migrated north and west to find the glowing promises unfulfilling. Over one and a half million left the South between 1950 and 1960. The Supreme Court ruling of 1954 opened a Pandora's box in race relations.[68]

Bellamy's greater contribution was as an ambassador of goodwill. He knew how to bring people of different races and cultures together, for he had done so in Oklahoma with whites, blacks, Hispanics, and Native Americans. He was ideal for the job. In 1957, Bellamy brought Dr. Victor T. Glass to the Atlanta office to assist him with administrative work. Upon Bellamy's retirement in 1964, Glass became the director in 1965. He brought in Dr. Wendell R. Grigg in 1966 and Emmanuel McCall in 1968. When McCall came in 1968, he had decision-making powers and shared an office with the rest of the staff.[69]

When Glass became department director in 1965, he also brought Arvella Turnipseed to his office as secretary. She was

---

Ibid., 136.
[68] Ibid., 136.
[69] Ibid., 137.

the first black in a non-staff professional role, aside from the custodians.

The Rutledge Years, 1965–1976

History proves that the greatest strides in racial inclusiveness in the Home Mission Board were made during the years when Arthur B. Rutledge was executive secretary-treasurer (president). A very quiet man, he was a mobilizer, motivator, and strategist. He clearly understood that the Home Mission Board had the largest staff of any Southern Baptist agency in the United States. He also understood the gravity of the racial polarization. He knew that the soul of the SBC rested on its resolution of racism. The staff and field personnel (2,266 persons)[70] understood how serious he was about this. The staff meetings, missionary assemblies, and various gatherings were times when we were informed, discussed, planned, strategized, and dealt with this reality.

Dr. Rutledge allowed us to have freedom. We could do what we felt best in fulfilling our program assignments as long as we were responsible for our own actions. There were times when staff members were challenged by pastors, denominational leaders, and laypeople who disliked any mention of race. If we were right in our statements or actions, Dr. Rutledge stood with us. A good illustration of this follows.

The Home Mission Magazine. Crucial to the success of the Home Mission Board during the Rutledge years was the *Home Mission* magazine, later called *Missions USA*. This monthly publication told the mission story, featuring missionaries, churches, institutions, laypeople, denominational staffs, and

---

[70] Ibid., 247.

anyone who was involved in kingdom work. Social customs, traditions, and attitudes were challenged. It was on the "cutting edge," an expression used in those days for being out front. The magazine became a model that other SBC denominational publications tried to emulate.

Walker Knight and his staff (Everett Hullum, Dallas Lee, and Don Rutledge) had the freedom to write about and photograph whatever they saw that would benefit the Home Mission cause. The magazine was always informative, but hard-hitting. Knight belonged to the Oakhurst Baptist Church, Decatur, Georgia. This church was itself in the forefront of community action and change. It was ahead of most other Baptist churches in its openness, its ministries across racial and social lines, its creativity, its missions giving (per capita), and just about any other measure one might use. Those looking for a church "engaged in the world" were drawn to Oakhurst. Several Home Mission Board staff belonged to the church, where they felt free to do experimental ministries.

Quite often, Knight drew criticism from pastors, churches, and SBC leaders because of the forthright approach of the magazine, but the subscription cancellations did not stop his resolve. The largest number of cancellations came after the January 1967 issue. The front cover featured a full-length picture of Dr. William Holmes Borders, pastor of the Wheat Street Baptist Church, Atlanta. Wheat Street initiated many community ministries that have been duplicated across the nation. These were featured for their informational value. The same issue carried an article about what black and white pastors in Louisville, Kentucky, were doing to effect racial recon-ciliation. Subscription cancellations came in the hundreds. Knight's organizational leader wanted him fired. Dr. Rutledge stood by him. The inter-level leader was removed. The encouragement from Dr. Rutledge and Knight's own personal fortitude did not diminish his resolve. There were other Southern Baptists who were anxious to see the refreshing content of the magazine. As word about it spread, it became the most sought after SBC publication, winning many awards among publication guilds and organizations.

The *Home Mission* magazine was perhaps the most effective communication piece that caused Southern Baptists to become more open and sensitive to racial reconciliation. It was followed by the WMU mission educational curricula.

The Department of Work with National Baptists

By SBC program assignment, the Department of Work with National Baptists led the SBC in its programs relating to African Americans, especially through National Baptist conventions units. This includes the three National Baptist conventions that existed from 1957 to 1995 (the National Baptist Convention, Inc., the National Baptist Convention of America, and the Progressive National Baptist Convention). The Christian Life Commission, organized in 1947, carried the assignment of race relations since it was involved with ethical concerns. Because the Department of Work with National Baptists had a field staff that at one time numbered 230, and the Christian Life Commission did not, the two worked together. The Christian Life Commission produced written materials and structured conferences that both units used to their advantage. They were interdependent.

The progress of Southern Baptists in race relations can be seen in the name changes of this department. In 1963, it was called the Department of Colored Work. That changed to the Department of Negro Work in 1965. In1968, it became the Department of Work with National Baptists. In 1972, the name was changed to the Department of Cooperative Ministries with National Baptists. In 1978, it changed to the Department of Black Church Relations. In1988, it became the Black Church Extension Division. Each name change reflected the continual nudge to get Southern Baptists away from paternal attitudes to fraternal and cooperative postures that respected the worth and dignity of African Americans and their organizations. The last name change admitted the lack of interest that National Baptists had in working with Southern Baptists, and the new direction of Southern Baptist interest. That interest was in relating to the openness of Southern Baptist associations and state conventions to receive black churches into their memberships and to intentionally start churches in predominantly African-American communities. The increasing number of black graduates of Southern Baptist colleges and seminaries fostered an openness to start new churches since many of them could not go to already established churches. Southern Baptists then began paying more attention to black churches in its ranks. That number is now in excess of 3,500. Some of them are dually aligned with a National Baptist convention as well as the SBC.

This black church relations program also resourced other Home Mission Board programs and agencies of the SBC. There was continual partnership with the Woman's Missionary Union, the Sunday School Board (now called Lifeway), the Christian Life Commission (now called Ethics and Religious Liberty), the Commission on the American Baptist Theological Seminary (now defunct), the Foreign Mission Board (now the International Mission Board), and the six Southern Baptist theological seminaries. These entities took seriously the mandate of the 1968 Statement on the Crisis in the Nation and sought to find ways for their agencies to implement the charge.

Other Programs of the Home Mission Board and Racial Reconciliation

The Home Mission Board had twelve official programs, as authorized by the SBC. Not all of them lent themselves to specific work related to racial reconciliation. Those that did included Christian Social Ministries, Special Mission Ministries, Language Missions, Evangelism, Chaplaincy, Church Extension, and Missionary Personnel.

Missionary Personnel Division. The Missionary Personnel Division had a demanding but meaningful role. They advocated for missions as a vocation, received applications, screened applicants, recommended those for appointment, and helped the sending programs to care for missionaries in service.

This division also had a pivotal role in racial reconciliation efforts. As associations and state conventions began seeing the need for the appointment of indigenous missionaries in the various communities, this division had to help locate people from various ethnic groups and blacks to seek appointment. That was not an easy task. Native Americans, Hispanics, and blacks were not particularly interested in being identified with the SBC because of its past. This division joined the others in calling attention to Southern Baptists about the image, perceptions, and actions that were offensive to non-Anglos. There were times when the division personnel had to be forceful with those who were racially insensitive. The "sending" programs intensified their efforts in appointing non-Anglos.

As a result, many African Americans, Hispanics, and Native Americans were appointed. Originally they were appointed to serve in areas of their own ethnicity. As Southern Baptists became more accepting, they served across racial and ethnic lines. In the secular world, this is called "crossover." The Home Mission Board's appointees began serving based on gifts and abilities, not ethnicities.

This division also made a recommendation to Dr. Rutledge that was a tremendous boost in ethnic recognition in the SBC. The division suggested that we change the format at Home Mission Weeks at the summer assemblies for one year. Instead of the usual Bible study in the mornings and a preacher in the evenings, they asked that we give major ethnic groups the day and let them plan the worship convocations. Each major group—African Americans, Hispanics, Native Americans, European ethnics, Pacific Asians, and the deaf—had a day to plan worship in their own identities. This concept was later done in state conventions and associations. Even churches began inviting ethnic and black churches in their area for similar experiences. The significant thing this did was to help Anglos begin to appreciate other worship styles. Eventually, they became more accepting of other people.

Christian Social Ministries. The Christian Social Ministries Department promoted the work of Baptist centers, halfway houses, homes for pregnant women, children's homes, hunger ministries, homeless ministries, crisis counseling, juvenile rehabilitation, migrant ministries, adoption ministries, literacy, and disaster relief. All of these crossed racial lines. This department saw to it that discrimination was not allowed even in the Deep South. The Christian Social Ministries staff at the Home Mission Board was very conscientious about applying the gospel in their actions. Often they dealt head-on with those in local situations that were racially immature. Their advocacy was a strong catalyst in racial reconciliation. During my years I

relied heavily upon Paul Adkins, Beverly Hammack, Charles
McCullen, Mildred Blankenship, Jewell Beall, Clovis Brantley,
and Bill Amos.

Special Mission Ministries. The Department of Special
Mission Ministries gave attention to volunteer missions,
Student Summer Missions, Mission Service Corps, and
innovative missions. They often worked with the National
Student Ministries office at the Sunday School Board in
relating to college students. Discussions about race relations
often came up at the various student conferences and
gatherings.

In the 1960s and 1970s college students were at the
forefront of changes in our society. They saw through the
sham of some Christian professions and initiated change.
Student Weeks at Ridgecrest and Glorieta Baptist Conference
Centers usually featured thought-provoking speakers,
conferences, and programs, stirring students to action when
they returned home.

Special Mission Ministries started church missions trips
where groups interested in doing something special could go to
other parts of the nation and do mission tasks. People from the
Deep South would travel, at their own expense, to northern
states, building churches, repairing homes, remodeling
tenement housing, while doing backyard Bible studies, worship
services at night, or other forms of evangelism. This program
was at first criticized heavily. Why would someone travel
across the country at their own expense when the same needs
they were addressing could be done at the home locations?
The strategy was to get people out of their environment to
"open their eyes," to become sensitized to others, and to see
that the same needs existed at home. The strategy worked.
People returned with new awareness, new skills in relating to

people, new perspectives in dealing with their own prejudices, and a new determination to minister in their settings.

Much credit goes to Warren Wolfe and Don Hammonds for their leadership in encouraging Southern Baptists to see the need for employing blacks and ethnics in mission positions.

Language Missions. The Language Missions Division ministered to all people for whom English was a second language. They also ministered to the deaf. Originally this ministry was directed toward Native Americans. It, along with the ministries to the slave population, was the immediate reason for the organization of the Domestic Mission Board. As Southern Baptists expanded out of the South, ministries to more language groups developed. In 1991, Southern Baptists were ministering to more than ninety language groups in the United States. This led both C. Peter Wagner and R. Pierce Beaver, as cited in the introduction, to say that the SBC was the most diverse religious body in the United States.

The Language Missions Division had to do more than minister to those who spoke languages other than English. They also had to minister across cultural, ethnic, social, and racial prejudices. Both Language Missions and Black Church Relations often partnered in emphases and approaches to challenge racism in the SBC. Ironically, both Oscar Romo (Language Missions Division) and Emmanuel McCall were elected to lead their respective divisions in the same meeting in 1973. This marked the first time that non-Anglos directed SBC programs. Also interesting is the fact that opposition to our elections came from some who worked in our programs. They thought that only Anglos should continue to lead SBC programs.

Oscar Romo, Irvin Dawson, Fermin Whittaker, and Gerald Palmer (the earlier division director) addressed the problems of racism related to both ethnics and blacks. These men developed strategies for helping churches and individuals become racially and ethnically inclusive.

Evangelism Division. Evangelism is at the very heart of the SBC. Like the conflict with Peter and the Jerusalem Council in the book of Acts, the battle raged in the SBC about who would be evangelized and how. What was to happen to those who were evangelized but were not Anglo?

Southern Baptists were influenced by various sources. Dr. Billy Graham insisted that his rallies be open to all people, without exception. When Dr. Kenneth Chafin came to the Home Mission Board as Director of Evangelism, having worked with Graham, he brought with him that same insistence. He took the initiative to add African-American staff to help train everybody to reach everybody.

A second influence that pushed Southern Baptists was the negative reports from missionaries and mission fields. Those that were being evangelized in other nations were appalled at what they saw and heard in the news and what those who came to America reported when they returned. A great deal of thanks goes to the missionaries who, during their furloughs, pleaded with Southern Baptist churches to deal with their racism and negativities.

A third impact came from students who won classmates and friends to Christ, but could not bring them to church. The number of varied responses from collegians would fill a book, such as having alternative worship on the lawns of the church at the same time worship was going on inside, refusing to participate in church or organizational activity until all were included, and other various ways of protesting discriminatory practices. These were often embarrassing to church or denominational leadership, as well as parents.

Nathan Porter and John Havlik were staff whose pronouncements regarding racial inclusiveness did much to help reconciliation.

Southern Baptists were also impacted by those who responded to their evangelistic efforts only to be denied full participation in the life of the church or organization. Dr. Arthur B. Rutledge used his authority in both screening potential staff and in leading sensitivity training for all staff. There were persons turned away from the Home Mission Board because of their racial immaturity. The ability to lead people to faith in Christ and to nurture them was key to his purpose in our staff. This was also expressed in the other two programs that I have only mentioned—chaplaincy and church extension. These programs were charged to minister to all people. During the discussions about the Homogenous Unit Principle (focus on reaching your kind of folk), the Home Mission Board was very clear: "Everybody is our kind of folk." Thus, racism in the SBC became a direct and indirect target of all we did. Dr. Charles Chaney, a vice president for the Missions Section, dealt head-on with the Homogenous Principle and led Southern Baptists to discard it.

M. Wendell Belew

I want to mention Wendell Belew separately. When I came to the Home Mission Board in 1968, Belew was Director of the Church Extension Department. He later became director of the Missions Division.

Belew established a relationship with me immediately upon my arrival. He was living in an area of racial transition, but had a firm commitment to stay put. He and John Havlik helped develop a community organization to ease racial tensions and transitions. Belew not only invited me to look at vacant homes in his community, but when I chose a home two blocks from him, he took a week of vacation to help me prepare the home for occupancy. Living in the same neighborhood allowed us to carpool when possible. When Belew became Missions Division Director, my department was in his division. This placed us as partners as well as neighbors.

Belew was the Home Mission Board's undesignated strategist. He birthed creative ideas that helped us have the strongest mission program of any denominational agency. When we went to the American Society of Missiology meetings, other denominations were eager to hear what we were doing. They depended on us for new ideas. Southern Baptists earned a new respect from other denominational staffs.

Belew also helped Southern Baptists to be open to listening and exchanging ideas with others. He helped Southern Baptists rise above provincialism.

Belew was very popular with the Woman's Missionary Union. I often was programmed in Woman's Missionary Union events with him. As he moved toward retirement, I inherited some of the confidence that the Woman's Missionary Union had in working with the Home Mission Board.

I will never forget a Woman's Missionary Union Week at Glorieta. Wendell and I were programmed together and separately. Our responsibilities were during the mornings and evenings. Our afternoons were free. On two afternoons we went to the Pecos National Monument. Wendell was an artist, while I dabbled with photography. He indicated things that he wanted pictures of. While he drew sketches, I photographed. He took my photos from which he made other art pieces. One of those pieces hung over my fireplace mantle for years. I donated it and other art pieces to the museum honoring him by Kentucky Baptists.

Wendell has never been properly recognized by Southern Baptists nationally. His genius is to be found in much of the creative and innovation mission programs that Southern Baptists had. I had the privilege of delivering his eulogy. He was perhaps my closest friend in Southern Baptist life.

The Program of Black Church Relations

Between 1965 and 1975, the program emphasized reconciliation through cooperating with National Baptists at the association, state convention, and national levels. Two things changed that focus: (1) National Baptist leadership was not interested. They saw it as an attempt to steal churches; (2) the increasing number of black churches joining the SBC or started by the SBC demanded more attention and services. Desperately needed in the SBC was an increased awareness of overcoming racism and how to relate to others who were different.

The Program of Black Church Relations was able to get its counterpart departments in state conventions to join in the awareness efforts. Our state directors were most effective in setting up race relations conferences in various regions of their states. The Program of Black Church Relations began writing and publishing, through the Home Mission Board and Broadman Press, the materials needed for reconciliation ministries. The Christian Life Commission partnered with emphases, materials, and conferences on reconciliation.

I would be remiss if I did not mention by name the staff and state directors who were used by God in these efforts: Victor T. Glass, W. R. Grigg, Edward Wheeler, Carlisle Driggers, Chan Garrett, William (Bill) and Margaret Perkins, Willie McPherson, Bobbie Murphy, Michael Cox, J. D. Ellis, and Sandra Hill, all of the Atlanta, Georgia office; Jack O'Neal, Tom Kelly, California; Elmer Whiten, Northwest Convention;

Bob Lovejoy, Oklahoma; Corbin Cooper, North Carolina; William T. Moore and Eugene Bragg, Michigan; Robert Ferguson and Jack Kwok, Arkansas; W. P. Davis and Richard Brogan, Mississippi; Thomas Pfeiffer, Harvey Hoffman, and Jimmy Brossette, Louisiana; H. O. Hester, Billy Nutt, and Wyndel Jones, Alabama; Durwood Cason, Earl Stirewalt, and Edward Davies, Georgia; Ernest Mehaffey and Pat Johnson, South Carolina; William Rogers and Lincoln Bingham, Kentucky; Phil Rogerson, Virginia; Julius Avery, Larry McCullough, and Larry Elliott, Florida; H. Wesley Wiley, Paul Clark, and Roy Godwin, District of Columbia; W. Paul Hall, Tennessee; Loren Belt and William Givens, Missouri; James Norman, Illinois; Ron Rogers, Maryland; Jim Goodner, New Mexico; Hal Crane, Pennsylvania; Thomas Davidson, Ohio; Judy Rice, Alaska; Darwin Farmer and James Culp, Texas.

These leaders co-opted interested pastors and laypeople to help them in promoting racial reconciliation. Resolutions were constantly before associations and state conventions. Local church, regional, and statewide conferences were held. The use of black preachers in the various levels of evangelism conferences opened the door to the giftedness of the black pulpit. Men often used included Fred G. Sampson, Manuel Scott, S. M. Lockeridge, Raymond Harvey, A. Louis Patterson, Sandy Ray, William Jones, E. V. Hill, Robert Wilson, and Harold Carter. There were others used occasionally, but these names usually drew Southern Baptist crowds.

A point of contention arose between black Southern Baptists and the frequent use of the above named men. They were all identified in one of the National Baptist conventions. Black Southern Baptists had good preachers that were not being used in those big preaching convocations. They also paid a stiff price for being identified with Southern Baptists. They felt they should have been heard. The Program of Black Church Relations used its opportunities to address this concern with state and associational leaders. Gradually, more black Southern Baptists began to be used.

Bob Banks. At the time when black Southern Baptists were requesting more assistance from the Home Mission Board, it was clear that reorganization was needed. The Program of Black Church Relations was included in that reorganization and given a higher profile. We were moved from a department to a division, given a larger responsibility and an added budget. Bob Banks, executive vice president, was the architect of the reorganization. We owe him a great deal of gratitude for understanding the need and raising the profile.

Partnering with the Sunday School Board. Dr. Sid Smith was employed by the Sunday School Board in 1979, first as staff in the Special Ministries Department, later as manager of the Black Church Development Section. The Program of Black Church Relations had to cease some of the services it provided to black churches that were really the responsibility of the Sunday School Board. With Sid having been a missionary of the Home Mission Board, the transition of those tasks was easy. Sid was included in all the programmed events of the Program of Black Church Relations. The Program of Black Church Relations also cooperated with his initiatives. There were times when we worked together to address problems related to other programs and agencies.

Sid initiated the idea of a black SBC fellowship that would be made up of church representatives. The fellowship would help the denominational agencies know of the needs of black churches and would provide opportunities for connectedness among the churches.

Sid later spirited networking among those blacks who were employed in SBC offices at whatever level. The organization was named the Black SBC Denominational Servants Network. Recognitions were given to those who merited such at an annual meeting preceding the SBC meeting.

Sid was followed by Rev. Elgie Wells. Wells began what is called Black Church Week, a week of intense training, alternating between the Ridgecrest and Glorieta Conference Centers. This week addresses the particular needs of black churches, but also serves to introduce them to the resources available in the SBC.

Mr. S. E. Grinstead and National Student Ministries. One of the early catalysts for change in the SBC were the events surrounding the National Baptist Student program. Student work was the domain of the Sunday School Board, but because this program related to the black community, the black student staffs were appointed and employed by the Home Mission Board.

Mr. Scott Edward Grinstead was the BSU director for four black colleges and universities in Nashville: Fisk, Meharry Medical School, Tennessee Agricultural & Industrial Institute, and American Baptist Theological Seminary. He was first employed by a joint committee of National and Southern Baptists in Nashville. That program began July 10, 1945.[71]

In 1953, Grinstead was appointed by the Home Mission Board as the first national BSU director for historically black campuses. Grinstead traveled to these colleges and universities developing BSUs. At the time of his retirement in 1968, fifty-six campuses had vital BSU programs. This began at a time

---

[71] Ibid., 138.

when campuses were not integrated. Grinstead developed the National Baptist Student Retreat, a weekend gathering of black BSU students from across the nation. At times the attendance reached 1,600. Many of the students who participated in the BSU program later became prominent leaders in various walks of life.

Grinstead was also the first black to be allowed to stay on the Ridgecrest Baptist Assembly campus. When he started attending Student Week meetings in 1947, he stayed in private homes in Black Mountain, North Carolina, the town nearest Ridgecrest. In an interview that appears in *Speaking to the Mountain*, Grinstead said he endured the inconveniences of discrimination only because his goal transcended them.[72]

Dr. Clarence Jordan, founder of the interracial community "Koinonia," at Americus, Georgia, frequently spoke at Student Weeks. He noted the inconveniences Grinstead was enduring and invited him to speak to the audience one evening. Jordan continued speaking out for change. The administration resisted. The next year, when Drs. Hugh Brim of the SBC Christian Life Commission and Benjamin E. Mays, president of Morehouse College, had to stay at the nearby Warren Wilson College and drive back and forth to Ridgecrest, change came. The assembly grounds opened to everyone.[73]

Following Grinstead's retirement, the Home Mission Board provided interim leadership for student work for two years. The Sunday School Board then decided to include all

[72] William T. Moore, *Speaking to the Mountain* (Atlanta GA: Home Mission Board, 1982) 70.

[73] Chan Garrett and William T. Moore, *Speaking to the Mountain* (Atlanta GA: Home Mission Board, 1982) 67.

student-related emphases in the National Student Ministries program. Reverend John Westbrook was employed to consult with the black colleges and universities and to help other campuses minister to black students. The black student directors wanted to continue the National Baptist Student Retreat for traditional reasons. Reverend John Corbitt, one of the former student presidents of the retreat, provided leadership. In 1976 the specific emphases related to black campuses were taken over by the National Baptist Convention, Inc.

Again, white students deserve much credit for sensitizing their parents, denominational leaders, and the general public to the injustices of racism and for pressing for change. Student emphases on both the local and national levels usually presented those program personalities who were thought-provoking and challenging. The students were willing to act on their convictions. They helped change to come. We must applaud the student directors and program leaders for being courageous and risking their jobs to be creative.

End of an Era

In October 1991, I took early retirement from the Home Mission Board to pastor a new congregation, the Christian Fellowship Baptist Church. (Early Retirement meant I had completed twenty-five years of service with the Home Mission Board, though I was not sixty-five.) Reverend Willie McPherson, a staff associate, was named my successor. Shortly thereafter, the SBC reorganized. The Home Mission Board became the North American Mission Board. The programs of the North American Mission Board were also restructured.

A Vignette

"Moses Wasn't a Southern Baptist"

The Southern Baptist ministers in a particular state had an annual golf tournament each spring. The picture of the player with the best score and the winning team always appeared on the front page of the weekly state paper.

The editor of the paper, the State Director of Student Ministries, and another pastor felt it was time to integrate the event. They invited a black pastor-friend to join the foursome. Knowing that the event director would object, they registered him, but did not reveal his identity.

On the day of the tournament, the group picked up Moses Javis. The golf course was a private country club. When Moses appeared, attempts were made to stop his play. The editor raised the possibility that the pastors might not want their actions in the next issue. The tournament leaders decided to let him play. After all, "he couldn't win at a 'white man's game'. No harm would be done."

But wouldn't you know, Moses' team not only won the tournament, but he had the best individual score. The next dilemma was, "We can't put his picture on the front page of our state paper, but how can we get around it?" Someone remembered a technicality: "Moses wasn't Southern Baptist. After all, this was a Southern Baptist ministers' tournament."

However, the editor was a courageous friend. The picture of the winning team did appear on the cover. A notation gave Moses' winning score. Moses later left that state to pastor in Missouri and Florida, where he recently retired. He conducts an annual golf tournament for ministers and laypeople, "The Saints and Sinners Golf Classic." For a

whole week, those who attend golf during the day and at night attend seminars on various aspects of church life.
A Vignette

"Mr. President, Please!" Home Mission Staff Luncheon, September 1968

Monthly At-Home Weeks were times when the entire staff of the Home Mission Board was expected to be in the office. Our time was spent reporting, accounting, planning, building team spirit, and doing anything else for the good of the organization. A staff luncheon was usually held on Wednesdays. At that time we heard from our Executive Director. He might also bring in other denominational leaders as appropriate.

The president of the SBC was always invited to the September luncheon and to the Home Mission Weeks at the summer assemblies. The Home Mission Board Weeks at Ridgecrest, North Carolina, and Glorieta, New Mexico, were very special times for the entire mission force, pastors, and lay leaders. The attendance often averaged in excess of 2,500 at each place.

At the September staff luncheon the new SBC president, a prominent pastor, was the speaker. He began by telling an "ethnic" joke. Most of the 126 persons present responded in silence. A few snickered. He tried it again. That time, twenty-one of us rose to leave. A Hispanic brother and I were the only ethnics in the room. As we arose, Dr. Rutledge went to the microphone and asked us to show courtesy and not leave. He explained to the speaker that we didn't consider ethnic joking funny and asked him to refrain from it. Later in his speech, he did it again. This time Dr. Rutledge did not restrain our leaving.

The invitation for the president to speak at our Home Mission Weeks had already been affirmed. Dr. Rutledge again reminded the brother of what was considered appropriate. On the first night of the week, he did it again. Most of the staff came to the evening assembly only for the promotional and inspirational parts of the service. We left before the preaching, as did some of the missionaries. The evening sessions were miserable failures as far as the preaching.

The Glorieta, New Mexico, Home Mission Week followed two weeks later. The president conveniently "took ill." Select Home Mission Board staff preached. It was a good week.

Chapter 12

Woman's Missionary Union:
The Compassionate Partner

Only the Lord knows the full extent of the contributions women have made to racial reconciliation in the SBC. Much of it was voluntary service. Some of it was in organizational programmatic influence. Significant partnerships were formed with women in National Baptist Convention churches and associations. Black women began participating in Woman's Missionary Union annual meetings as early as 1895.[74]

The program assignment affirmed by the SBC in 1888 for the Woman's Missionary Union was missions education and financial support for the two mission agencies. The seeds for nurturing more meaningful relationships had already been sown. Slave women worked in the homes of white women who were Southern Baptist. Despite prohibitions against it, some women taught their slave women to read, write, and other domestic skills. Some did so seeing their slaves as "mission opportunities." Some did so to lessen their own work. A few had the uplift of the race as a goal. Samuel Hill suggests, "Placed as plantation wives were in close juxtaposition to

---

[74] Catherine Allen, *A Century to Celebrate: History of the Woman's Missionary Union* (Birmingham AL: Woman's Missionary Union, 1987) 242.

slaves, responsible for their physical and spiritual well-being, many southern women became secret abolitionists. When the Civil War came it was not uncommon for women to view it as God's punishment of the South for the sin of owning slaves. Women often described emancipation as the will of God."[75]

Following the Civil War, some southern white women developed supportive relationships to offset the activities of northern Baptist missionaries who had come south to help develop the newly freed people.[76] Whatever their motive, bonds were formed between black and white women that allowed Southern Baptist women to continue patterns that led to racial sensitivity.

Early in the Woman's Missionary Union history, the influence of Nannie Helen Burroughs opened the way for progressive relationships between black and white women that are sustained throughout its history. Burroughs organized women in the National Baptist Convention in October 1900, aided by Annie Armstrong, the corresponding secretary (executive leader) of the SBC Woman's Missionary Union. Burroughs was corresponding secretary of the Woman's Auxiliary of the National Baptist Convention until 1948. She continued as president until 1961.[77] Her persuasive forcefulness and dynamic personality helped posture Southern Baptist women to be open for ministries of racial reconciliation.

Through the years the Woman's Missionary Union developed social service programs in black communities, promoted funding for training black Baptist women, featured

---

[75] Samuel S. Hill, *Religion in the Solid South* (Nashville TN: Abingdon Press, 1972) 93.

[76] Allen, *A Century to Celebrate*, 242.

[77] Ibid., 244.

black women in their *Royal Service* magazine (Burroughs was the first in 1947), and integrated its Woman's Missionary Union training school in Louisville, Kentucky, in 1952. The Woman's Missionary Union of Virginia appointed the first black staff person, Ms. Fletcher Howell, in 1934.[78]

The writer's first awareness of the Woman's Missionary Union came in 1957, as a student intern at the Baptist Fellowship Center in Louisville, Kentucky. This center was a joint project of the Long Run Baptist Association (white) and the Central District Baptist Association (black). My assignment was to develop Royal Ambassador organizations in the Central District churches. My internship was paid by the Woman's Missionary Union through the Home Mission Board, SBC. A second part of my assignment was to help conduct interracial activities for boys from both associations. This was at the beginning of school integration talks in Louisville. The joint committee that oversaw the work of the Baptist Fellowship Center took an initiative for teaching racial reconciliation as part of the mission education content.

In 1957, the *Long Bridge* mission study book was released. The study of this book precipitated a conflict between the SBC Executive Committee, which did not want the book released, and the Woman's Missionary Union, which produced the study book and wanted it used. While the Woman's Missionary Union was respectfully obedient, there were those who went ahead with the study. The study book, which had already been printed, somehow made its way to those churches

---

[78] For a fuller picture of the activities before 1957, the reader is invited to read Allen, *A Century to Celebrate*, 241–57.

that were loyal to the Woman's Missionary Union. I have
already treated this event earlier in the book.[79]

The Home Mission Board, for whom the mission study
was done, partnered with the Woman's Missionary Union both
in the publication of the book and in the struggle to get it to
the churches. Their mutual efforts began to forge a supportive
alliance for future tasks. Not only did they share similar views
about the need for racial reconciliation, but they supported
each other in actions to accomplish that end. Ms. Alma Hunt,
who led the Woman's Missionary Union as executive secretary
from 1948–1974, and Dr. Arthur B. Rutledge, who led the
Home Mission Board from 1965–1976, became allies in
leading their organizations to the forefront of racial
reconciliation ministries. The reader should know that Hunt's
passion for racial reconciliation was fueled not only by her
earlier influences, but also by the refusal of the deacons in her
membership church to allow blacks to worship there in the
1960s. She was also angry that she could not carry on the
normal contacts with her friends of color, both American and
international, due to the restrictions of that day.[80]

In 1967, the Woman's Missionary Union included
scholarships for National Baptist collegians and seminarians as
a part of the Annie Armstrong Easter Offering promotion.
That year, 179 scholarships were granted. They were
dispensed through the Department of Work with National
Baptists at the Home Mission Board. This ministry grew out of
two concerns: the embarrassment that blacks could not earlier
attend Southern Baptist schools and that scholarship resources

---

[79] Ibid., 254.

[80] Alma Hunt, *Reflections from Alma Hunt* (Birmingham AL: Woman's
Missionary Union, 1987).

were scarce. The Woman's Missionary Union's efforts were added to by those of state conventions. By 1975 more than two million dollars annually went to scholarships for National Baptist collegians and seminarians preparing for full-time ministry:

> During the 1960s WMU women had to find creative ways to continue their work and relationships with Black people in order to skirt personal endangerment from those who intensely disagreed with them. There were those who privately joined the Civil Rights efforts. Some by driving women to work during the Montgomery bus boycott. Some by joining the Church Women United who opposed the Arkansas governor during the Little Rock school crisis. Mildred McMurry (WMU executive secretary) served on the Birmingham mayor's committee concerning school desegregation. Although these were probably the most difficult years of race relations, these were probably the years that the women of WMU truly began to understand sisterhood among the races.[81]

This helps us understand the momentum behind the 1968 SBC action that produced the Statement Concerning the Crisis in Our Nation. Mrs. Marie Mathis (national Woman's Missionary Union president), Ms. Alma Hunt, and the state Woman's Missionary Union leaders rallied the support for the passage of that document. The statement, mentioned earlier,

---

[81] Betty Williams, "Woman's Missionary Union: From Uplift to Sisterhood" (unpublished student research paper).

helped refocus and galvanize the SBC and its agencies toward positive actions in racial reconciliation.

Beginning in 1965, the Woman's Missionary Union began preparing "how to" books, providing practical help for areas of crisis and need. There were "Mission Action Guidebooks" for drug and alcohol addiction, poverty, hunger, English as a second language, relating to immigrants, etc. There was also a guidebook to help Anglos know how to properly relate to African Americans. The Home Mission Board's Department of Work with National Baptists and its missionary force of about 230 people were in constant demand to teach that emphasis in Southern Baptist churches and associations.

A later vignette, "I Will Loan You One of My Dresses," references a plane trip to Springfield, Missouri. Ms. Carolyn Weatherford and I met in St. Louis to transfer to the Ozark flight to Springfield. We were both on program at the Missouri State Woman's Missionary Union Annual Meeting. During that wait for the connecting flight, Weatherford, who was the successor to Hunt, raised the idea of our joint partnership in a staff position at the Woman's Missionary Union to be filled by a black woman. This person would help the Woman's Missionary Union direct its relations and resources with National Baptist women and develop Woman's Missionary Unions in the black churches that were joining the SBC. The position would be housed at the Woman's Missionary Union in Birmingham. The staff person would be paid by the Home Mission Board and available to assist the Department of Black Church Relations ministries.

The process and budgeting were in place by 1978. Mrs. Margaret Perkins was hired for that position. Her husband, William (Bill), was already on our staff. Margaret fulfilled her role beyond our expectations. We were not prepared for the fact that she became so popular that the Anglo churches, associations, and conventions were asking for her time. Her assignment was revised to allow her to be a generalist, rather than confined to one area. This reflected a change that is now common in all of the SBC programs. African Americans are assigned by skills and needs of the organization, not to relate only to African Americans.

Since 1995 the Woman's Missionary Union has continued to expand its offerings and exert its influence in racial reconciliation. Because of the limitations of the book, someone else will tell that story.

The leadership of the Woman's Missionary Union in dealing with racism, nationalism, regionalism, and class separatism continues to be felt not only in the states of its influence in America, but around the world. When the SBC withdrew from the Baptist World Alliance (2003), the Woman's Missionary Union stayed. It had influenced women around the world with mission zeal and would not abandon its sisters in Asia, Africa, Europe, and South America. It is very present in matters related to women's issues: abuse, class separatism, racism, economic depravity, social slavery of various kinds, educational depravation, unjust systems, ancient customs and traditions. The list goes on and on.

This writer is of the firm conviction that in the American South, the women not only made the difference, but prompted the men to take seriously their social responsibility.

A Vignette

"Walking with Miss Alma," Spring 1970

The Woman's Missionary Union has, from its beginning, been an organization that emphasized ministries of love and reconciliation. Its leaders have known how to move around the objections and obstructions of SBC leadership and do the caring, loving, and reconciling work that needs to be done.

In 1965, the Woman's Missionary Union began producing a series of guidebooks designed to help churches minister to various situations. They also did guidebooks to help individuals and churches relate to the various ethnic and racial groups.

When I began at the Home Mission Board in 1968, I was invited to help write the book relating to blacks. The constant communication and interaction between the Woman's Missionary Union and myself allowed some relationships of mutual trust to develop. That trust was to prove itself in early 1970 while attending the SBC Executive Committee meeting in Nashville. The out-of-town guests stayed at the Andrew Jackson Hotel. I was late coming down from my room to attend the evening session. In the lobby was Miss Alma Hunt, executive director of the Woman's Missionary Union. It was already dark, and she was afraid to walk the two or three blocks to the SBC building alone. When she saw me she asked if I would walk with her. When I consented she took my arm and off we went. The only concern I had was that it was 1970. Black men would be arrested, or worse, if seen in the presence of white women. But I was not afraid. If anyone objected, Ms. Alma knew how to put them in their place.

We walked the three blocks with her taking my arm all the way. When we arrived at the SBC building, the meeting had not begun. Those standing and talking on the outside and in the halls looked, some with consternation, others with amusement. Ms. Hunt and I both nodded and spoke to them and went into the building. Once inside, she started to go on her own to her desk in the front of the assembly hall.

Then, with a twinkle in her eye, she said, "Please escort me down the aisle to my desk." I did. If eyes were knives, I would have been shredded to pieces. Long before there was *Driving Miss Daisy*, I walked Ms. Alma.

A Vignette

"I Will Loan You One of My Dresses," April 1977

I was invited to speak at the Missouri Woman's Missionary Union meeting at Springfield. My plane went from Atlanta to St. Louis, and then transferred to a commuter plane. Ms. Carolyn Weatherford, then executive director of the Woman's Missionary Union, had flown from Birmingham to St. Louis. During the wait we had time to discuss plans for the projects that we were mutually involved with. One of them involved the Home Mission Board funding a black staff person in the Woman's Missionary Union who would relate to both organizations.

When we arrived at Springfield, a mature couple was there to meet us. They were delighted to have the privilege of bringing program personalities to their hotel and the convention. Unfortunately, my luggage did not arrive on the same flight with me. We were told it would be sent on the next flight, arriving at 6:00 P.M.

Carolyn and I sat in the back seat as we were taken to the hotel. I was lamenting the fact that I was dressed casually in slacks, a turtleneck, and sweater. Such attire would have been inappropriate for a main speaker at a Woman's Missionary Union meeting. Knowing this, I asked Carolyn's advice on my options if my luggage did not arrive. Neither of us knew where we were scheduled in the service for that evening.

Seeing that I was ill at ease, Carolyn tried to calm me by saying, "Don't worry, Emmanuel. If your luggage does not come in time, I will loan you one of my dresses." While we laughed, the dear couple up front was confused. They looked at each other, and then back at us. I still remember the eyes of the driver through the rearview mirror. Fortunately, my luggage arrived in time for me to dress appropriately and attend the service.

A Vignette

"He Hugged a Kleagle," February 7–10, 1970

Laypeople deserve much credit for doing unusual things to help bring about racial reconciliation in the SBC. Frank Graham of Graham, North Carolina, was one such person. He was the Associational Director of Missions. As a layman, he felt secure in doing whatever he thought. He came up with the idea of having a joint associational revival. The local black association had agreed. The three featured program personnel were Dr. Vance Havner (a very popular Bible teacher); Mr. J. Robert Bradley, a National Baptist musician; and myself.

Just prior to the meeting that was to have lasted a week, the local Ku Klux Klan sent out word that created fear in the minds of most blacks and some whites: "Anyone attending that meeting would be dealt with." The first two nights, the attendance averaged between sixty and sixty-five. Only one black lady showed up. She didn't get the word.

Bob Bradley had a knack for getting the congregation to participate in the singing. It was a common practice of his to come down the aisle singing, shaking hands, hugging, or anything else he felt like doing. On the third night, the service was "cold." The reason was the local kleagle (KKK leader) had come in and sat at the back to observe those in attendance. The local people knew him. Havner, Bradley, and I did not. Havner was first on the program with his Bible study. Bradley was sitting on the other side of the front. He bounded to the podium when Havner finished. Frank Graham tried to get his attention, but failed. Graham turned to me and said, "When you go up to the pulpit, whisper to Bradley that we might have trouble tonight. The kleagle is here. Be ready for anything."

I moved even more quickly to the pulpit. As I went to whisper in Bradley's ear, he moved aside and down the steps to the aisle. Once on the floor he stopped the singing and said, "Now, you all aren't singing with the spirit. I want only the ladies to sing this next verse. Darlings, if you sing it right I am going to give everyone of you a big kiss." (Remember, there was only one black woman in the room.) When that verse ended, Bradley noticed the one man in the back by himself. As he was singing he walked right up to the man and extended his hand. When the man refused, Bradley, a very robust man, grabbed him and hugged him. The man ran out of the building.

Frank Graham came up to the pulpit and put the congregation at ease. He had posted plain-clothed security around the church in case there was a problem. J. Robert Bradley still did not understand what had happened until we reviewed it on the way back to the hotel. Then he was overcome with fear. We decided to cancel the other two nights!

Chapter 13

The 1995 SBC Resolution on Racial Reconciliation

The years following the 1976 bicentennial of our nation saw several apologies for previous wrongs. In 1992, the 500th anniversary celebration of Christopher Columbus's coming to America lost much of its luster as various groups apologized to the American Indians for the various wrongs done to them. Others, such as the Southern Baptist Alliance and the Cooperative Baptist Fellowship (splinter groups of the SBC), apologized to African Americans for previous injustices. The Lutherans apologized to Jews for the Holocaust and for Martin Luther's reference to Jews as "Christ killers." Pope Paul led Catholics to apologize to Africans and Czechs for the wrongs done to them in their countries.

Some of those apologies may be by-products of the conscience-raising of Mr. James Foreman. On Sunday, May 4, 1969, Foreman, a leader in the Student Non-Violent Coordinating Committee, interrupted the Sunday worship of the Riverside Church, New York City, and read his "Black Manifesto." The document had been discussed at the Interreligious Foundation for Community Organization meeting, April 25–27, 1969. This was a conference for religious and denominational leaders, community organizations, Civil Rights organizations, and anyone else interested in the plight of black Americans.

Dr. Gayraud Wilmore[82] suggests that it was the preamble of the "Black Manifesto" that drove white and some black participants from the meeting. Its references to guerrilla warfare, a socialist society, and revolutionary control caused alarm. His tactic of disrupting a Sunday morning worship service was also extensively criticized by blacks and whites.

The manifesto condemned America for its racist past, for not having kept its promise to the newly freed slaves (to give each family forty acres and a mule), for having stripped blacks of citizenship rights and decency. It made demands for reparation sums of up to $200 million for black economic development.

Often there are imitators who repeat highly publicized actions for whatever their purposes and reasons. This happened in some communities. Churches and denominational meetings were fearful of interruptions and disruptions. While the "Black Manifesto" and James Foreman were rebuffed by both blacks and whites, the matter of repairing damaged relationships and dealing with race and class discrimination moved higher on the agenda of religious groups. Making public apologies was seen as a necessary "first step" in the reconciliation process.

Southern Baptists had a number of responses to the Foreman action. The more positive response came at the annual SBC meeting, June 1969. Southern Baptists called upon all citizens to work for racial justice, economic improvement,

---

[82] Luther Copeland, *The Southern Baptist Convention and the Judgment of History: The Taint of an Original Sin* (Lanham MD: University Press of America, 1995).

political emancipation, education and Christian understanding.[83]

The 150th Anniversary of the SBC, June 1995

For several years prior to this historic date, there were those in the SBC who felt that some definite statement of apology should be made to African Americans in order to clear the air for further reconciliation and healing. In 1993 and 1994, resolutions had been presented to the Resolutions Committee on this theme. One was drafted by Rev. Penny Ellis, Birmingham, Alabama; Dr. Jere Allen, executive director, DC Baptist Convention; Rev. Mike Fahey, Baltimore, Maryland; and Rev. Delroy Reid-Salmon, Bronx, New York. Their efforts came out of a meeting in Atlanta, Georgia, in October 1993, when fifteen directors of associational missions, along with others who worked in metropolitan areas, met to address common concerns. Their document was circulated to Southern Baptist entities in the hope that a sentiment would be expressed in the 1995 convention. Several state Baptist conventions adopted their resolution or similar statements.[84]

Dr. G. Bryant Wright, a prominent pastor in Marietta, Georgia, also presented a resolution to the Georgia Baptist Convention in November 1994. He had encountered the animosity of the black Atlanta religious leadership when he tried to coordinate an area-wide revival crusade in preparation for the 1996 Olympics in Atlanta. The black pastors indicated their feelings about Southern Baptists and their intent not to cooperate even though the effort was across denominational lines. Wright's resolution was adopted and became an

---

[83] *Atlanta Constitution*, 14 June 1969, 6.
[84] "SBC Reconciliation Resolution Gets Mixed Reaction in Media," *Christian Index* (27 June 1995): 3, 5.

instrument used by the Georgia Baptist Convention Executive Director, Dr. J. Robert White, in his appeal to the two black state conventions in Georgia. The apology was warmly accepted.[85]

On May 9, 1995, the SBC Historical Commission celebrated the actual date of the founding of the SBC in the First Baptist Church, Augusta, Georgia. In that meeting, a declaration was adopted, stating that slavery was a "contributing factor to the formation of the SBC" and pledging "to publicly combat the sins of racism and exclusion in our communities." I reprint that document as it was adopted.

Declaration of Repentance and Rededication

Since its founding in 1845, the Southern Baptist Convention has been a leader in missions, evangelism, and social ministry. However, our relation to African-Americans has been less than ideal.

The issue of slavery and defense of the right to own slaves was a contributing factor to the formation of the SBC in Augusta, Georgia, in 1845.

At its roots, this defense of slavery was designed to preserve the material prosperity and way of life for white Southerners at the expense of African-Americans.

We recognize that the racism and exclusion which, plagues our culture today, is tied to the past and we must be continually willing to confront it anew.

---

[85] "SBC Resolution Expected on Racial Reconciliation," *Christian Index* (15 June 1995): 1, 8.

While we cannot undo the past, we desire to express our sense of grief for the injustice of our former days.

We acknowledge the historic role of Southern Baptists in condoning and perpetuating the sin of slavery before and during the Civil War and do hereby publicly apologize to all African-Americans for the sins of our ancestors.

We ask forgiveness from our brothers and sisters, and reject the racism, and prejudice which has persisted throughout our history as Southern Baptists even to this present day.

In doing so, we acknowledge that our own healing is at stake, that racism and the exclusion of others impedes our own development as a people and discredits the Gospel we proclaim.

We long to feel the joy of life lived in the fullness of Jesus Christ—a life freed of shame, restored to fellowship, and authorized by our Heavenly Father to be a redemptive and reconciling presence among all the peoples of the world.

We pledge ourselves to repentance in order to commit ourselves to be agents of Christ's reconciling peace and to publicly combat the sins of racism and exclusion in our communities.

God help us to learn from this tragic lesson and not repeat it by excluding others we think are different. It is our fervent hope and prayer—that by acknowledging and repenting of the sins of our past—we will be freed to live in justice and peace in the present.

In early 1995, Dr. Luther Copeland's book *The Southern Baptist Convention and the Judgment of History: The Taint of an Original Sin* was released. Copeland, a former missionary, then a professor of missions and ethics at Southeastern Baptist Theological Seminary, had been one of the persons who taught, spoke, and wrote about how racism had affected the SBC witness on the international mission fields. His basic thesis was that the internal problems and divisiveness in the SBC was related to its original sin of racism.[86]

On May 22, 1995, the SBC Christian Life Commission in Nashville, led by Dr. Richard Land, held a Racial Reconciliation Consultation. Sixteen persons, equally divided among black and white, gathered to draft what became the 1995 resolution. Reverend Gary Frost, an African American and first vice president of the SBC, was a co-chair with Land. We worked for hours refining the document to be presented. Key to our efforts was the politics involved. We had to be sure every word was genuine and sincere, but would not raise opposition from possible detractors. Drs. Albert Mohler, Paige Patterson, and Richard Land were extremely helpful here. They sensed those from whom opposition would come with the use of certain words or phrases. They knew the theologically and psychologically weighted areas for potential challenges. When the document was finished, they knew whom to approach to quell resistances. Here is the resolution that was presented to the 20,000 messengers in the Georgia Dome, June 20, 1995.

---

[86] Copeland, *The Southern Baptist Convention.*

Resolution on Racial Reconciliation on the 150th Anniversary of the Southern Baptist Convention

Whereas, since its founding in 1845, the Southern Baptist Convention has been an effective instrument of God in missions, evangelism, and social ministry; and

Whereas, the Scriptures teach that "Eve is the mother of all living" (Genesis 3:20), and that "God shows no partiality, but in every nation whoever fears him and works righteousness is accepted by him" (Acts 10:34–35), and that God has "made from one blood every nation of men to dwell on the face of the earth" (Acts 17:26); and

Whereas, our relationship to African-Americans has been hindered from the beginning by the role that slavery played in the formation of the Southern Baptist Convention; and

Whereas, many of our Southern Baptist forbearers defended the "right" to own slaves, and either participated in, supported, or acquiesced in the particularly inhumane nature of American slavery; and

Whereas, in later years Southern Baptists failed, in many cases, to support, and in some cases opposed, legitimate initiatives to secure the civil rights of African-Americans; and

Whereas, racism has led to discrimination, oppression, injustice, and violence, both in the Civil War and throughout the history of our nation; and

Whereas, racism has divided the body of Christ and Southern Baptists in particular, and separated us from our African-American brothers and sisters; and

Whereas, many of our congregations have intentionally and/or unintentionally excluded African-

Americans from worship, membership, and leadership; and

Whereas, racism profoundly distorts our understanding of Christian morality, leading some Southern Baptists to believe that racial prejudice and discrimination are compatible with the Gospel; and

Whereas, Jesus performed the ministry of reconciliation to restore sinners to a right relationship with the Heavenly Father, and to establish right relations among all human beings, especially with the family of faith.

Therefore, be it Resolved, that we the messengers to the Sesquicentennial meeting of the Southern Baptist Convention, assembled in Atlanta, Georgia, June 20–22, 1995, unwaveringly denounce racism, in all its forms, as deplorable sin; and

Be it further Resolved, that we affirm the Bible's teaching that every human life is sacred, and is of equal and immeasurable worth, made in God's image, regardless of race or ethnicity (Genesis 1:27), and that, with respect to salvation through Christ, "There is neither Jew nor Greek, there is neither slave nor free, there is neither male nor female, for we are all one in Christ Jesus" (Galatians 3:28); and

Be it further Resolved, that we lament and repudiate historic acts of evil such as slavery from which we continue to reap a bitter harvest, and we recognize that racism which yet plagues our culture today is inextricably tied to the past; and

Be it further Resolved, that we apologize to all African-Americans for condoning and/or perpetuating individual and systematic racism in our lifetime; and we genuinely repent of racism of which we have been guilty, whether consciously (Psalm 19:13) or unconsciously (Leviticus 4:27); and

Be it further Resolved, that we ask forgiveness from our African-American brothers and sisters, acknowledging that our own healing is at stake; and

Be it further Resolved, that we hereby commit ourselves to eradicate racism in all its forms from Southern Baptist life and ministry; and

Be it further Resolved, that we commit ourselves to be "Doers of the Word" (James 1:22) by pursuing racial reconciliation in all our relationships, especially with our brothers and sisters in Christ (1 John 2:6), to the end that our light would so shine before others, "that they may see (our) good works and glorify (our) Father in heaven" (Matthew 5:16); and

Be it finally Resolved, that we pledge our commitment to the Great Commission task of making disciples of all peoples (Matthew 28:19), confessing that in the church God is calling together one people from every tribe and nation (Revelation 5:9), and proclaiming that the Gospel of our Lord Jesus Christ is the only certain and sufficient ground upon which redeemed persons will stand together in restored family union as joint-heirs with Christ (Romans 8:17).

The resolution was presented by Dr. Charles Carter, pastor of Shades Mountain Baptist Church, Birmingham, Alabama, who served as chair of the Resolutions Committee. The meeting was presided over by Dr. Jim Henry, pastor of First Baptist Church, Orlando, Florida, and convention president. Dr. Henry began this part of the business with remarks about the seriousness of what we were about to do, followed by a time of prayer.

The resolution was discussed for twelve minutes. Only three speakers opposed the motion. The question was called for, and the vote was at least ninety-five percent favorable according to those assigned to observe.

Following the vote, President Henry called the vice president, Gary Frost, to the podium. After embracing, Frost represented the African-American constituency by accepting the resolution and challenging the SBC to live up to its commitment. This was followed by a season of prayer and thanksgiving. Convention messengers gathered in small groups for the prayer. Gary Frost closed the "season of prayer." One could not help but notice the African Americans scattered throughout the auditorium holding hands with their nearest white neighbors.

The reactions to the resolution were predictable. Blacks in the SBC saw it as a movement to a higher level. They had an instrument to use as leverage if their associations or state conventions seemed to be in default. Some found greater acceptance by the cooperating churches when they returned home. Whites attempted to fulfill the commitments by seeing that more people of color were placed on strategic boards and committees in denominational structures. Some churches seemed more eager to cooperate with others in racially changing communities, even opening their facilities for use at alternate times. Some Churches that were dying made their properties available at reduced prices. Some gave them to the new residents of the community.

African Americans outside the SBC wondered if the resolution was a trick or ploy to enlarge SBC numbers by soliciting more African-American churches. Previous opinions and suspicions about Blacks in the SBC seemed to reinforce a threatened negativism.

The secular press, who had covered too many stories that fed their suspicions, was also divided about the Southern Baptist resolution. The *New York Times* (New York), *Chicago Sun-Times* (Illinois), *Akron Beach Journal* (Ohio), *Orlando Sentinel* (Florida), *Houston Chronicle* (Texas), the (Memphis) *Commercial Appeal* (Tennessee), *Fort Lauderdale Sun-Sentinel* (Florida), the (Jackson) *Clarion-Ledger* (Mississippi), *St. Louis Dispatch* (Missouri), *Atlanta Journal* (Georgia), and *Louisville Courier Journal* (Kentucky) were among the papers that wrote positively about the SBC action. Carl T. Rowan, a popular black syndicated columnist, wrote an open letter to President Jim Henry, calling the resolution "a genuine expression of godliness."[87]

A Vignette

"On Their Knees, Praying for Me," Spring 1969

The Mississippi National Baptist Student Retreat, an annual event involving more than 600 black college students, was being held at the Sophia Sutton Baptist Assembly, Prentiss, Mississippi. I was to speak three times, the first being Friday evening.

On Friday morning, W. P. Davis called to say that he would not be able to meet my plane at Jackson. The registration was more than expected and he had to go down early. I was to rent a car, get directions, and come to the assembly.

---

[87] "SBC Reconciliation Resolution," 3, 5.

My plane left Atlanta two hours late due to mechanical problems. I arrived in Jackson just after dark. The drive to Prentiss would take about two hours. I was concerned, remembering W. P.'s earlier experiences of being beaten by "night riders." The back roads of Mississippi were not safe then.

I got lost after leaving the main highway and wandered around for at least an hour before I came to a crossroads grocery store that had black people around it. I was afraid to stop anywhere else. They gave me directions to Prentiss, where reservations awaited me at the one hotel in town.

I arrived at about 9:00 P.M. An unruly rodeo crowd was in front of the hotel. When I entered, some not-so-friendly faces immediately confronted me. When I gave the clerk my name, she affirmed my reservation, greeted me, and gave me the key to my room. I went directly to my room and bolted the door. About 9:30 P.M., I remembered that no one at the assembly knew of my whereabouts. I was to have spoken at that evening's service.

I returned to the front desk, asked for directions to the assembly grounds, and started the brief journey. When I walked in the door, I saw the more than 600 students and their leaders on their knees. They were praying for my safety!

Chapter 14

New Kinds of Challenges

I am now involved in three kinds of challenges related to interracial inclusiveness and cooperation. I am national moderator of the Cooperative Baptist Fellowship (CBF) and pastor of a new congregation that is sharing space with a predominantly Anglo congregation. Let me discuss each separately.

I became involved with the CBF in its infancy because I believed in the values it espoused: the respect for the free Baptist tradition, democratic participation both in the national fellowship and the local church, the primacy of missional cooperation, and historic Baptist principles.

Not many African Americans know about the CBF. It is not because of any racial or prejudicial feelings; in fact, many of those who fought the racial battles in the SBC are now in the CBF. I believe we have a great movement. I am doing what I can to help inform the African-American community to "check us out." I am convinced that the missional activity of our cooperative efforts, the hospitality of our local congregations, and the holistic education at our partner seminaries will help us tell the story that African Americans can find a place of purpose and commitment in the CBF.

The second challenge is what brought me out of pastoral retirement. As often happens, groups in Baptist churches disagree. Sometimes the disagreements are serious enough to cause division. There is an old cliché: "Baptists multiply by dividing." That happened to the Christian Fellowship Baptist Church. One of the divided groups asked me to come out of retirement and lead them to solidity. Because of my love for them, their proven missional commitment, and the possibilities that I saw, I joyfully agreed to become their pastor.

The First Baptist Church, East Point, Georgia, is a church that was struggling with community transition. They had space available for us to share the facility at the same time. This we began to do on Sunday, August 6, 2006. We are using the sanctuary and other space for offices, classrooms, etc. They are using the regular office space, the chapel, and the classrooms they need. Fortunately for us, their pastor and I were classmates in seminary. We remained in touch through the years. When Charles Worthy retired from the Pennsylvania Avenue Baptist Church in Washington, D.C., he returned to Jonesboro, Georgia, the community next to us. He and Caroline worshiped with us regularly at Christian Fellowship. They would have joined had they not known of my plans to retire. In the providence of God, Charles was called to First Baptist, East Point, Georgia. He and the church made it possible for our new church, the Fellowship Group, to share their space. Now we are planning joint activities that will facilitate the growth of both churches and give a strong witness in that community. The future is very bright.

The third challenge is serving as a vice president of the Baptist World Alliance. There are twenty-one vice presidents representing the Baptist World Alliance in various regions of the world. I am enjoying my tasks of serving with the Study and Research Executive group, chairing the Human Rights Award committee, and assisting President David Coffey and

General Secretary Denton Lotz. I have been involved in the
Baptist World Alliance since 1976. I have served as Chair of
the Ethics Commission and as a member on other committees
and commissions. In July 1996, I chaired the Baptist World
Alliance participation in the Olympics. In January 1999 I
hosted the International Summit on Racism and Ethnic
Cleansing in Atlanta.

In July 2005, the Baptist World Alliance, an organization
of more than 211 Baptist conventions, associations, and
fellowships, celebrated its centennial—100 years of cooperative
efforts for the kingdom of God. As more than 13,000 of us
gathered in Birmingham, England, we experienced an event
that would take volumes to tell. I can summarize it by speaking
of the joy of seeing people cross races, cultures, social strata,
languages, church practices, theological differences, and any
other barrier to express our oneness in Christ. We sat side by
side in general sessions, in seminars, small groups, at eating
places, at the various venues made available. Love, peace, and
harmony flowed as we sang, prayed, listened to the preached
word, and engaged in several kinds of Bible study. Those
blessed with more of life's goods shared with our brothers and
sisters who came to the meeting without adequate resources.
Plans were made by units other than the Baptist World
Alliance to engage in cooperative actions to help evangelize,
disciple, teach, and resource other churches and conventions.
We experienced true "Koinonia."

Every time I have gone to a Baptist World Alliance
General Council Meeting or Executive Meeting, I come away
rejoicing, for I have had a foretaste of what heaven will be like.
Nowhere in his word has God indicated that heaven will have
any segregation of any kind. We will gather from all nations,

kindred, tribes, and tongues. Our oneness will be reflected in the word "redeemed."

I affirm the words of an old spiritual in the black tradition:

> When all God's children get together,
> What a time! What a time! What a time!
> We're going to sit down at the Welcome Table,
> What a time! What a time! What a time!

Bibliography

Books

Allen, Catherine. *A Century to Celebrate: History of the Woman's Missionary Union*. Birmingham AL: Woman's Missionary Union, 1987.

Barnette, Henlee. *A Pilgrimage of Faith: My Story*. Macon GA: Mercer University Press, 2004.

Beaver, R. Pierce, editor. *American Missions in Bicentennial Perspective*. Pasadena CA: William Carey Library, 1977.

Bennett, Lerone. *Before the Mayflower: A History of the Negro in America, 1619–1954*. New York: Penguin Books, 1966.

Copeland, Luther. *The Southern Baptist Convention and the Judgment of History: The Taint of an Original Sin*. Lanham MD: University Press of America, 1995.

Day, Richard Ellsworth. *Rhapsody in Black: The Life Story of John Jasper*. Valley Forge PA: Judson Press, 1953.

Dorough, Dwight. *The Bible Belt Mystique*. Philadelphia PA: Westminster Press, 1974.

Eighmy, John Lee. *Churches in Cultural Captivity: A History of the Social Attitudes of Southern Baptists*. Knoxville: University of Tennessee Press, 1972.

Fletcher, Jess C. *The Southern Baptist Convention*. Nashville TN: Broadman Press, 1994.

Goddard, Terry. "Southern Social Justice: Brooks Hays and the Little Rock School Crisis." *Baptist History & Heritage* (Spring 2003): 68–85.

Hill, Samuel S. *Religion and the Solid South*. Nashville TN: Abingdon Press, 1972.

Holmes, Thomas J. *Ashes for Breakfast*. Valley Forge PA: Judson Press, 1969.

Hunt, Alma. *Reflections from Alma Hunt*. Birmingham AL: Woman's Missionary Union, 1987.

Jordan, Winthrop. *White Over Black: American Attitudes Toward the Negro, 1550–1812*. Chapel Hill: University of North Carolina Press, 1968.

Lincoln, C. Eric and Lawrence Mamiya. *The Black Church in the African-American Experience*. Durham NC: Duke University Press, 1990.

McBeth, H. Leon. *The Baptist Heritage*. Nashville TN: Broadman Press, 1987.

McCall, Emmanuel. *Black Church Lifestyles*. Nashville TN: Broadman Press, 1986.

Mitchell, Henry H. *Black Church Beginnings*. Grand Rapids MI: William B. Eerdmans Publishing Company, 2004.

Moore, William T. *His Heart Is Black*. Atlanta GA: Home Mission Board, 1979.

Raboteau, Albert. *Slave Religion: The Invisible Institution in the Antebellum South*. London: Oxford University Press, 1978.

Ragsdale, B. C. *The Story of Georgia Baptists*. Atlanta GA: Executive Committee of the Georgia Baptist Convention, 1938.

Rutledge, Arthur B. *Mission to America: A Century and a Quarter of Southern Baptist Home Missions*. Nashville TN: Broadman Press, 1969.

Sapp, Phyllis. *The Long Bridge*. Atlanta GA: Home Mission Board, 1957.

Sernett, Milton. *Black Religion and American Evangelicalism*. Metuchen NJ: Scarecrow Press, 1975.

Shurden, Walter B. *Not a Silent People*. Nashville TN: Broadman Press, 1972.

Smith, H. Shelton. *In His Image, But...: Racism in Southern Religion, 1780–1910*. Durham NC: Duke University Press, 1972.

Sweet, William W. *Religion on the American Frontier: The Baptists.* New York: Cooper Square Publishers, 1964.

Wagner, C. Peter. *Your Spiritual Gifts Can Help Your Church Grow.* Glendale CA: G/L Publications, 1979.

Wheeler, Edward. *The Uplift of the Race: The Black Minister in the New South: 1865–1902.* Lanham MD: University Press of America, 1986.

Wilmore, Gayraud. *Black Religion and Black Radicalism.* Maryknoll NY: Orbis, 1983.

———, editor. *African-American Religious Studies.* Durham NC: Duke University Press, 1989.

Periodicals

"SBC Resolution Expected on Racial Reconciliation." *Christian Index*, 15 June 1995, 1, 8.

"SBC Reconciliation Resolution Gets Mixed Reaction in Media." *Christian Index*, 27 June 1995, 3, 5.